The Dream Net

Gathered, edited and with contributions
by
Miller H Caldwell

Clink
Street

Published by Clink Street Publishing 2022

ISBN:
978-1-915229-65-6 - paperback
978-1-915229-66-3 - ebook

*This book is dedicated to all Alzheimer's victims and their
wonderful carers.*

*All Royalties of this book will go to the Alzheimer's Society, united
against Dementia.*

You may say I'm a dreamer
But I'm not the only one
I hope someday you will join us
And the world will be as one

IMAGINE BY JOHN LENNON

FOREWORD

For centuries, people have questioned the meaning of dreams. Early civilisations thought of dreams as a medium between humans and the gods. The Greeks and Romans were convinced that dreams could predict the future. Since then, times have changed of course. Now there are many different medical theories and studies into dream meanings and dream interpretation.

What happens while we dream?

Dreams are essentially stories we play out in our heads, usually overnight. They can follow a linear narrative or be abstract or surreal. Scientists estimate that we have roughly three to six dreams in one night and around 95% of these dreams are forgotten the following morning.

Why do we dream?

Dreaming occurs during the REM (Rapid Eye Movement) cycle of sleep. During REM sleep, your eyes move quickly in different directions. Usually, REM sleep happens 90 minutes after you fall asleep. You tend to have intense dreams during this time as your brain is still active.

Professional dream analyst and author, Lauri Quinn Loewenberg, explains: 'Dreaming is a thinking process. In fact, it is a continuation of your thoughts from the day; the chatter in your head that goes on all day long.'

Once you enter REM sleep those thoughts continue in symbols and metaphors instead of words. During REM the brain is working differently to when we are awake. Certain parts of the brain have become dormant, such as the prefrontal cortex which controls rational thought, while other parts become highly active, such as the amygdale, that part of the brain that controls emotions. Through the dreaming process, you continue your thoughts about your day, your mistakes, your achievements and your hopes for tomorrow. Your dream thoughts are actually more focussed and significantly more profound because your dreams provide you a metaphoric commentary on yourself. Daydreaming recollections can be even more vivid and are included in this collection.

I have been delighted to receive so many literary contributions from friends and acquaintances throughout the world and from different backgrounds. Thus, this book is a collection of short dream stories, poems, commentary and dreams surreal and dreams true to life. There are no chapters. But your book mark will stride through the pages at a great rate. A short and sometimes longer CV is followed by the entry. Now, let the dreams come your way…now that they are caught in my net. MC

The Bait

This was the text which attracted contributors from all over the world. My Dutch friend Hannie Rouweler and Leicester-based journalist Andrew Goss were particularly instrumental in tracking down some very interesting international entries on my behalf.

We all dream. Something like 95% of dreams is forgotten. Many dreams take place shortly after going to sleep, when the brain is still active. Other dreams come to us shortly before we rise. I actually am one of only 5% of the population who recalls my dreams on waking.

I am looking for contributors to supply their own dreams. They can be short or long, surreal, factual, imaginative, wishful-thinking, poetic too, in fact, ANY DREAM WILL DO.

You may say I am a dreamer

But I'm not the only one.

I look forward to what you might provide. Send your dream to: netherholm6@yahoo.com

Thank you
Miller

The Royalties of this book go to the Alzheimer's Society, united against Dementia.

ACKNOWLEDGEMENTS

Some read the Acknowledgements after reading a book. To do so re-enforces the author's sources and inspiration, perhaps. But I suspect most will read about where my thanks are due before being transported to the world of dreams and dreaming. Is your bookmark ready? For there are no chapters.

I have many I must thank. A friend who is a retired chemistry teacher sent me a scientific dream. Like some others, he preferred not to be mentioned by name. Their requests are honoured while their contributions much appreciated.

Ann Massey, who works as editor at Spooky Isles, is a freelance writer and conducts Irish Paranormal Investigations. Thanks Ann, for your revelation.

Christina Scholz from Berlin provides the only German contribution but coming from the land of fairytales, her dream and artwork in the Fairy Dream is captivating. Thanks too Christina for 'The Search for Happiness'. Vielen Dank.

Pamela Faye runs a film company in Australia. Thanks for your sound advice Pamela.

To Stuart Clark and Alan Collins I am grateful for their local insight.

Poet and lecturer Kevin McCann brings a broad Lancastrian accent to his romantic tale. His poetry flows gracefully like the river Nith. His Christmas Eve story is one of the longer contributions and its festive theme is towards the end of the book. Much appreciated, Kevin.

Martin Greenlees brings us an alternative dream thought. Thanks, Martin.

Chrys Salt MBE has the Alzheimer's charity in mind with her two dream poems – The Alzheimer's Waltz, will thrill our older readership and may get them up to dance. Very creative, Chrys.

Hannie Rouweler is a Dutch poet whose works are internationally acclaimed. I was glad to have hosted her in Scotland and performed with her on Skye. Thanks for your contribution, Hannie and your efficient networking.

Dr Debra Drown, a resident of Vermont, is a clinical psychologist in New Hampshire and a dear friend. Keep dreaming, Debra, it's therapeutic I am convinced.

Jess Bart is Debra's daughter. Her insightful dream is unique and much appreciated.

Nicola Sharp is a retired child psychiatrist and writer who lives in nearby Cumbria. Thanks for your insight at the table, Nicola.

Rick Hale describes himself as an American author living near Illinois, a cancer survivor, an amputee, an old school ghost hunter and a Domestic God. I am delighted to know you and your prolific work, Rick. It is a significant contribution, as anticipated.

Thanks too to the enigmatic Russian, Eldar, for his thoughts and his report of being a Covid 19 patient in a Siberian hospital.

From Kyrgyzstan, Rahim Karin Karimov, translator and award winning poet, brings a fresh selection of his internationally acclaimed work to the pages. Рахмет Рахым. (Thanks once more, Rahim.)

Catherine Czerkawska is a well-known Scottish author who has provided an interesting dream about fact. She is a novelist, historian and experienced professional BBC playwright, living in rural south Ayrshire. Well done Catherine.

Marion de Vos-Hoekstra is a Dutch Ambassador's wife, translator and a published poet worldwide. Marion, thank you very much for your contribution. I enjoyed reading your poetry very much indeed.

Andrew Goss is a Leicester-based humanitarian and journalist and brings us a dream from India. Pakistan means a lot to both of us. His book *The Humanitarian* is a fascinating story about his life in Pakistan. Andy also gives us a taster of his latest book, *Cold Coffee and Bananas*, in 'A Touch of Fever'. Your dreams are gratefully received, Andy.

From Bulgaria comes **Rozalia Alexandrova sending her GIFT for you. I am delighted to have discovered you, Rozalia.**

Representing India is Gurpreet Dhariwal, the author of *My Soul Rants*. She contributes her poem Diary of a New World, for you to reflect on. Delighted to have you on board, Gurpreet.

Also from Leicester comes John Coster bringing us One More Day. Many thanks for the video interview John.

Merryn Glover writes fiction, drama, poetry and journalism. In a life spent crossing cultures, she was born in Kathmandu and brought up in Nepal, India and Pakistan. She went to University in Australia, keeps returning to South Asia, but has called Scotland home for over 25 years.

MathildeVuillermoz's brother Paul was tragically killed. She dreams about him often. She is my former film director. Our final external contribution comes from Belgium's Joris Iven, a distinguished poet, internationally acclaimed, and my good friend.

Of course, I apologise to my wife for my tossing and turning in bed as my dreams unfold. She is most forgiving, I am glad to report. With you everything is possible; without you I cannot imagine.

Finally, our daughters, Fiona and Laura. I have no intention of embarrassing you too much, so I will just tell you how much I love you.

Contents

Miller Caldwell has led a humanitarian life in Ghana, Pakistan and Scotland. He began full time writing in 2003 after falling ill. Recently his work has found favour with film directors and his editor and publisher, Mandy J Steel Collins at Beul Aithris, adds her magical dust to his current work.

The Glasgow Bus

Glasgow awoke from its usual dowdy, cloudy drizzle to shed sunshine all over the green city that afternoon. I had been visiting my blind cousin Brian who lives near the Great Western Road, in the city, and whose memory is amazingly accurate. He can tell which car I have had in the past in ordered sequence and he inquires if the latest has had its first service. Blind since birth, he lives in a universe of mechanics and family.

I lived in Glasgow many years ago but was now living in Blackwaterfoot on the beautiful island of Arran, in my mind. I was heading home. I had in my satchel a novel, *A Lingering Crime*, and I had also purchased an *Evening Times* should the train journey south to Ardrossan require a crossword to fill.

From boarding at Kelvin Bridge subway station, I alighted at Buchanan Street station and then crossed over to Renfield Street and onward to the Central railway station. I was in good time. I was not in a hurry. Pedestrians passed by at a good rate on their purposeful errands.

Yellow and green, the colours of Glasgow transport in obviously partisan colours had their buses plying up and down Renfield Street.

I was aware of a bus slowing down and indeed it stopped just ahead of me. I think three passengers alighted. A man around forty years of age with a thread of a black beard around his chin walked back up the street; an older woman with a head of blue-rinsed hair and a warm royal blue scarf, took her time to leave the bus and finally a woman carrying two bags. I caught a glimpse of her child behind her. The bus's doors closed and the 38 bus route to Rouken Glen resumed its journey.

That was when, by instinct, I darted into the road chasing the bus. The child was suspended by a harness trapped by the closed doors. I banged on the side windows as I approached the child. The driver caught my eye and waved me away. He did not stop for passengers once the doors were closed and he had obviously not seen the child, nor heard its whimpers. I grabbed the dangling child and unclipped the safety clasp on her back. Instantly she broke loose into my arms as the bus continued on its way, with the trapped harness flapping like a streamer on a summer's day outing. My last sight of the bus was to see passengers on the near side with mouths open, remonstrating to the driver to stop but I knew I had saved that child from dreadful injury.

Then unexpectedly, as the bus was slowing down, I looked behind to see and hear the child's worried mother approach at pace, shouting hysterically. I felt a solid bang on the back of my head. I glimpsed for a second at the offending white van's wing mirror before I hit the ground. I held the child close to me in a firm embrace and fell on my back hitting my head against the road surface.

I think I was in the Glasgow Royal Infirmary for two weeks, it may have been longer. I had grown an untidy beard for sure and recalled my grandmother had been the matron of this hospital more than a century ago. A doctor was at the foot of my bed. He was obviously pleased to see I had recovered despite a heavy white bandage, wrapped around my head.

'Can I go home now?'

'Do you know why you have been in hospital?' he asked in a concerned manner.

'No,' I replied.

The doctor opened a newspaper which he held. He read to me. It seemed I had saved a child from death and her mother, seeing me on the road unconscious, had contacted the press after the ambulance and police. The papers jumped at the story and began a campaign for me to be given an award.

Instantly I found myself at Buckingham Palace. The room was large and many seats were regimentally set out. When my name was called I stepped forward. Prince Charles decorated me with some medal and, as it was pinned to my chest, I woke up. The pin seemed to have gone through my pyjamas and pained me. The dream was over. It was approaching 7:15 am. At breakfast time I told my wife about this dream.

I then sat down to remember many of my other vivid dreams which I have dreamt. I thought dreams might make an interesting book and so I asked some friends if they remembered their dreams. I asked if they could send them to me. The responses I got from all over the world were overwhelming, and wonderful, as you are about to discover. But first, it's time to meet my parrot, Kofi, for the first of my two parrot dreams.

The Precocious Parrot

The head teacher of Shiskine primary school, near Blackwaterfoot, on the island of Arran had invited me to speak to the children, bringing with me my African Grey parrot, Kofi, in this dream. I had actually owned the bird for a number of years in Ghana, West Africa, when I worked there. It had been my constant partner, before I was married.

The children were thrilled to see and hear the parrot answer many of my mundane questions. I encouraged them to come up and stroke the parrot's head but not its red tail feather as that was a sensitive spot. The last child to come up was a boy. I think I called him Bobby in my dream. I can't be sure. However as he lingered, I decided he could have Kofi perch on his arm. Clearly Bobby loved Kofi and was pleased to have been chosen to hold the parrot. He spoke to it and the parrot inclined his head. It understood his questions and replied appropriately. The class laughed as Bobby continued to ask the parrot questions until the mid-day bell rang. The children all stood up ready to play in the playground. But I had to apologise. It was not break time at all. The bell sound emanated from Kofi's beak. The class were in hoots of laughter. Five minutes later it was the real school bell and Kofi repeated its tone as soon as the janitor had stopped ringing his clanger.

I was invited into the staff room where Kofi fascinated the teachers, twiddling a ginger nut biscuit like a card trickster in his claw. They sat drinking their Bolivian coffee. I was given tea, my preference.

Then all hell broke loose. It began with a voice approaching the staff room, it was an angry mother. Her fist knocked on the staff door making it rattle. I thought she might break the frosted glass.

The head teacher went to open the door and I saw her take a deep breath in preparation for confrontation. She placed her hand on the handle and the door burst open. The woman continued to raise her voice in anger, as she advanced. It seemed Bobby, her son, had phoned his mother at break time and told her he had held a parrot in class. Straight away she made her way to confront the Headmistress, in her Paisley-patterned apron with her curlers still in place. The gist of her anger was that Bobby suffered allergies, particularly of feathers. His bed cushion was full of polystyrene marble-sized balls and not a feather ever entered their home. The woman accused the Head teacher of not recalling his medical notes. No Feathers. That bird had bloody F E A T H E R S, she spelled out. That bird had been very close to Bobby's face. Through sobbing tears the mother informed the open mouthed staff, that she was taking Bobby to the doctor, right there and then. She did not want to suffer another restless night with a child gasping for breath.

The atmosphere was tense in the staff room. Kofi sensed the atmosphere and said, 'Oh dear.' I finished my tea and left the Head and her staff to cry and comfort one another.

The next scene was to find a bouquet of flowers at my front door. There was no label on them and I had no idea who the kind person was who left them. Later that afternoon the front door bell rang. I opened the door to find an attractive woman in a summer dress with immaculate auburn wavy hair. I did not recognise her but I did recognise Bobby who stood beside her.

She told me she had sent the flowers as a peace offering. Apparently when the doctor sent the boy to the allergy expert at the hospital, they found Bobby was no longer allergic to feathers. It had been a doze of Kofi, my African parrot, which had been the answer. His feathers acted as a biological immunotherapy on Bobby and so his feather allergy was totally cured. She could not have been more excited or happy. I was pleased for her.

I got out of bed at 8:05 am feeling very satisfied at the result, no matter how improbable it might have been.

Ann Massey is editor of the *Irish Spooky Isles* and a freelance writer of Irish paranormal investigations.

Family Dreamers

I very occasionally have prophetic dreams. For example a recent one had me dream of a friend I had not spoken to in months, being in trouble. I messaged her as soon as I awoke. She replied, startled at my dream, to tell me she had been diagnosed with cancer. She's grand now, thank goodness. My daughter and my cousin get visits from loved passed ones in their dreams. It's kind of a thing in our family.

Miller H Caldwell

An enchanting children's story by Leicester author
Andrew Goss, with wonderful illustrations by
Christina Schulz in Berlin.

The Fairy Dream

ZAYD lay perfectly still. He was waiting, listening in the semi-darkness, eyes wide open as he peeped over the covers into the shadows. Everyone was in bed and in the quiet of the night he could hear the sound of his own heart beating. Thumpity-thump, thumpity-thump...

Through the gap in the curtains he could see the moon and the silvery light which shone into his room allowed him to see the shapes of his bedroom furniture.

But the longer he lay there, the more sounds he heard. The ticking of the big clock downstairs grew louder and louder. And the quicker his heart began to beat. Some of the shadows in his room took on monster-like shapes, so that he hardly dared look from beneath his covers.

Yet he was determined to stay awake, on this night of all nights, and pinched himself whenever he felt his eyes closing. Underneath his pillow lay the first tooth he had lost. It had 'fallen out' earlier that day and was now carefully wrapped in tissue paper, ready for the fairies to collect.

He had first felt the tooth wobble several weeks ago.

"You'll be getting a visit from the fairies soon," his Papa Nabil told his son with a chuckle and had smiled to see the excitement fill the boy's eyes.

"Do they really come out at night to fetch the tooth?"

"Of course," his Papa had said with a smile. "But only when the children are asleep, because they are frightened of big people."

"Oh," said Zayd. "Do you think I could see one if I stayed awake and was very still and quiet?"

"You could always try."

And this is exactly what Zayd had decided to do. Particularly as his Papa had been unable to tell him exactly what happened when a fairy came. When he asked his father again about the fairies, he had barely looked up from the newspaper which he read from cover to cover in the evenings. He was especially looking for news of Algeria, a country very far away on the very northern rim of Africa, where his Papa had lived as a boy.

"About the fairies..." Zayd began to ask him.

His father sighed heavily. Suddenly he looked very tired.

"Well... erm... I think... I don't really know. We can talk later. Run along. I'm busy right now," he had said with furrowed brow. He missed the country where he had grown up.

Zayd was surprised. His Papa usually knew everything. And he didn't see him later. Instead he frowned over the newspaper, sometimes sighing deeply and forgot all about the fairies.

If he could only stay awake to see what happened when a fairy came, maybe his Papa would stop reading the newspaper. Perhaps he would stop working so long every day in the shop, where every day dozens men and boys would come to have their hair cut.

Perhaps he would stop looking troubled. Perhaps he would listen. And maybe he would smile. He used to smile much more. Now he often seemed sad and tired when he came home from the shop. His Mama was the same.

But Zayd's tooth was at the wobbling stage only. Perhaps his sisters could help. Sukaina was 13 and wouldn't have anything to do with it.

"You'll just have to wait until it falls out," she said. She was already beginning to sound like a grown up. His sister Hajer was more helpful.

"Stand still, Zayd and I'll hit you in the mouth. I'll do it quick, so it won't hurt."

Zayd wasn't sure about this idea, but finally nodded in agreement.

"Wham! ouch!' Zayd screamed in pain and burst into a flood of tears. His Papa threw his newspaper down and stormed into the room. 'What is this?' he asked his children. He sent Hajer straight to bed without the usual supper. But Zayd thought the tooth was much looser after that and later smuggled a chocolate bar to his older sister. She was 11 and thought the idea of catching a fairy was pretty awesome. Only, she couldn't be bothered herself. Besides, she was impatient to get back to her computer games. Worse still, she was beginning to show an interest in make-up.

Zayd, however, was determined and twisted the tooth a little more every day for a week until finally it seemed to cling to his gum by a tiny thread. He went to find Hajer. One final twist and it was out! It hadn't hurt. That had been this morning.

"Are you sure the fairies will come tonight?" Zayd asked his Papa as he wrapped the little tooth carefully in tissue paper.

"Hmmm?" his father replied, as if he wasn't really listening.

"Will the fairies come?"

"Sure they will. That's what they say."

And Zayd slipped the small package under his pillow and bounced into bed, watched by his parents.

"Goodnight, Papa. Goodnight, Mama."

Then he yawned extra sleepily and turned onto his side, pretending to fall asleep immediately.

"Must be very tired," he heard his mother mumble on her way out.

As soon as she had left the room, Zayd put his finger to his mouth, just to make sure it had happened. He was happy to feel the gap, rubbing his fingertip over the ragged gum where the tooth had been. It was still sore, but had a reassuring numbness to it.

He wasn't certain how long he lay there. He must have dozed off, for the next thing he knew all the lights were out and the house was in complete darkness. Everything was still, except for the ticking of the big clock downstairs and the thumping of his heart.

He poked his tongue into the gap in his teeth, just to make sure. Suddenly he stopped what he was doing and listened as hard as he could. He was certain he heard a humming sound, like the buzz of a fly. He listened harder. It wasn't a fly. More like the quick flutter of a butterfly's wings. His eyes opened wider, peering bravely from under the covers into the darkness.

And then he saw it. A tiny dot of golden light which seemed to hover in the corner of the room, like a little firefly. Zayd kept perfectly still, his gaze resting on the dazzling light, desperate to breathe as quietly as he could. He felt his heartbeat quicken with excitement.

UNDER the covers Zayd pinched a small fold of skin between his fingers and squeezed firmly. The clock downstairs suddenly stopped ticking. He watched as the light came closer. What if the fairy should see he was still awake? He shut his eyes and kept perfectly still.

The grayness of his closed eyes became red, and then bright orange, as the light came closer. The flutter of tiny wings grew louder. And suddenly, they stopped. In the same instant he felt a little pat on the pillow beside his face, as if a tiny object had suddenly dropped beside him.

He opened his eyes slightly and found himself squinting at a little figure no taller than a matchbox, surrounded by brilliant light which lit the room like a candle. It had its back to Zayd and was much too busy looking for something to notice he was awake, as it struggled to slide its tiny arms underneath the pillow, tutting to itself like an angry bumble-bee.

It was quite the strangest creature Zayd had ever seen. It was dressed in sparkling yellow clothing which consisted of lycra mini-skirt, jacket, shiny golden tights and tiny heeled boots. The little head was a flame of blonde curls, through which Zayd could see pink pointed ears. And as it wriggled it threw out a golden dust from delicate wings upon its back, which began to fill the room like a cloud of glittering light.

Zayd felt a tickle on his nose and before he could stop himself shattered the silence with an enormous sneeze, sending his little visitor shooting across the bedroom like a firework across the sky, and into the far wall, sending sparks in all directions.

Zayd gasped. The little creature had fallen to the floor and its light had become weak and dim. What had he done? Curiosity overcame his sense of fear and he swung his legs out of bed and tiptoed towards the glowing light.

The dazed fairy rubbed her eyes in disbelief at the large child approaching. And pinched herself.

"You're not allowed to see me. You're supposed to be asleep," she said angrily in a squeaky voice barely louder than the quietest whisper.

"Sorry," said Zayd in reply and the fairy put her hands over her pointed ears.

"Shhhh! You're hurting my ears!"

"Sorry again," whispered Zayd. "Are you all right?"

The fairy nodded."But I'll have to put you to sleep right away," she said, whipping out a magic wand from a ruffle in her skirt. "Before you hurt me."

"But I won't hurt you and I don't want to go to sleep."

"I'm not risking it. I've seen what big people do to each other," said the fairy and performed a strange weaving motion with her wand. Nothing happened. She tried again, with a delicate sweep of her arm. The tiny wand was broken.

"Oh dear," said the fairy and tapped the little rod against the carpet, as if this might suddenly fix it.

"See what you've done," she added unhappily. "Now I simply can't do the magic."

Zayd smiled. "Good, because I want to see what happens."

"You don't understand, stupid. Not the sleep thing. Changing your tooth into silver coins. I can't take your great white tusk without performing the money magic. Now I'll never get the tusk back and without it I can't save the fairy city. And I am certain to become the last fairy."

Zayd was puzzled. "The last one?"

So the fairy explained.

Once upon a time, when Zayd's Papa was a boy, there were thousands of fairies and children's teeth were plentiful enough to build strong castles in the sky, high above the fluffy clouds where the great fairy cities floated on the four winds. Even above Africa. And especially above Algeria.

But a great tragedy had befallen the fairy kingdom. People had stopped believing in fairies. Children began to lose the magic of belief and give their dreams to new computer worlds. And their imaginations were being dulled by mobile phones. And every time a person stopped believing, a fairy dropped down dead. Great pearly white cities had fallen into decay and black storm clouds smashed the magnificent fairy castles. And the fairies were disappearing fast.

"Even when your older sisters stopped believing there were still many thousands of us. But now I fear I may become the only one. I haven't seen a fellow fairy for quite some time. And the city…" She began to cry. "The last city is falling into decay, threatened by the biggest, blackest clouds I have ever seen."

"Perhaps I can help," said Zayd and took the little fairy gently in his hand.

***

"We'll have to make our own magic," Zayd whispered, gazing intently at the little fairy resting on the palm of his hand. The tiny creature stopped crying and looked into Zayd's big brown eyes. Was a child capable of making magic? The fairy had heard such things were possible before children became too old and distracted to forget their dreams. The little figure rose to her feet and hugged one of Zayd's fingers gratefully.

"Do you know any spells, then?" asked the fairy.

"Only spellings from school, I'm afraid. And I'm still learning those. But I have an idea to create a different sort of magic, which just might help. Starting with the tooth." The fairy wasn't sure.

"You can have my tooth for nothing," said Zayd simply.

The fairy shook her head. "Couldn't possibly."

"Take it," Zayd insisted. "It will surely help to make the pearly city strong against the black clouds. You can have it. I don't need it."

But the fairy shook her little blonde head sadly.

"It's not possible. If I can't give you anything in return it makes me feel sad. And when I'm sad, I feel heavy. Then I'll never get off the ground. Fairies beat their wings on a tide of happiness they create whenever they make a wish come true – like leaving silver coins under the pillow. That makes for speedy flight!"

"Hmmm," said Zayd thoughtfully. And then he had an idea. He carried the fairy over to his pillow.

"It would make me very happy if you just took the tooth," he said.

"It won't work," said the fairy.

"Then why don't you give me something in exchange?"

"But I can't do the money magic with a broken wand."

"Then give me the wand – it's beautifully made and would make me very happy."

The fairy thought for a moment. It was true she had a collection of many different wands back at the fairy city. But letting a child have a magic wand – even a broken one – might cause problems.

Then again, it would create a necessary stream of happiness to allow the fairy to return to the city with the tooth. It was a tricky situation. But it might just work. And who would know? Yes, she convinced herself. It was the only way. She smiled and glowed so brightly the whole room was bathed in golden light.

"That would allow me to fly easily… if you're sure it would make you happy."

Zayd nodded. The fairy held out the tiny item, no bigger than a sewing needle and the little boy took it in his fingers, examining the delicate craftsmanship, as only fairies know how. It was sparkling silver with little golden stars which glittered and still gave off a little magic dust.

"It's a deal, then," said Zayd and the fairy darted quickly beneath the pillow for the precious tooth.

"I must get this back to the city above the clouds immediately," said the fairy, hovering in front of Zayd's face with the tissue package wedged beneath her arm.

"Will I see you again?"

The little creature nodded.

"Next time you lose a tooth… as long as you still believe." She sighed before continuing sadly: "If only there were more children like you. Then there would be more fairies and more magic in the world – and more teeth to make the fairy city safe against the darkest storm clouds."

"More magic. What do you mean?"

The fairy sighed impatiently.

"Don't you know anything? Fairies are responsible for granting wishes all over the world to help the Almighty. What do you think the pearly white city is for? It's not just for show, you know; it's the source of all fairy magic.

Now Zayd began to understand.

"Wait," he said. "You mean if the fairy city falls from the sky, no more wishes can come true?"

"No magic, no wishes," replied the fairy. "This internet thing has made everything so much more difficult. People have to imagine – and dream – to create the magic that binds the universe together. Don't you know anything?"

Zayd felt he did know quite a bit. But what the fairy said sounded sad.

"You see the problem," the fairy added.

"So it all depends on people believing," mumbled Zayd, echoing the fairy's sadness. And he felt he knew it was true. The fairy nodded.

"Suppose somebody was able to make lots of people believe in fairies?"

"I'd grant them their fondest wish, that's for sure," said the fairy.

Then it reached out its tiny hand to shake Zayd's little finger.

"I've got to fly now. But thanks for your help."

The little fairy disappeared in a puff of golden smoke before Zayd even had time to utter the word 'goodbye' and suddenly found himself sitting in the dark. But he could still feel the tiny wand he held between his fingers. And Zayd had another idea. He smiled at the thought of what the next day would bring as he closed his eyes and fell into a deep and comfortable sleep.

***

WHEN Zayd awoke the sky was already ablaze with the orange glow of the morning sun, peeping over the city rooftops. The familiar sound of the Blackbirds twittering outside his window nudged him from a deep sleep into the new day.

He raised himself in bed and stared bleary-eyed into the morning light which shone through the gap in the curtains. What a strange night it had been – and what a dream! It had seemed so real.

But wait. What about the tooth under the pillow? Had the tooth fairy really been? Quickly he tossed his pillow aside to look. His eyes widened. The tissue package in which it had been wrapped really was gone. He decided he had better go and see his mama and papa.

Zayd swung his legs out of bed, but stopped as soon as he lowered his foot onto the carpet and felt a sharp little stab against his heel. And there it was the tiny broken wand the fairy had left...

Pamela Faye is the owner of the Australian film studio Rolling Seas, an Australian company deeply entrenched within the movie industry.

Never give up on a dream.

As for the Dream Book, my only suggestion for Dreams is, "Never Give Up On A Dream" anything is possible in this world of ours and once the pandemic has passed, the world will want to charge ahead again.

A VISIT TO LARGS, AYRSHIRE

Miller Caldwell

Ann's story reminds me of an incident in 1968 when I lived with my family in Glasgow. It was not my dream but my mother's. She had a vivid dream that night and she told my older sister the following morning, to make our own family meal without her, at the end of the day. She had to travel.

I remember that evening meal. It was cod in a white parsley sauce, with mashed potato. My sister, Joan, made the meal and it was eaten in silence as we tried to come to terms with our mother's sudden disappearance. My mother's mother, my grandmother, was in a care home in Ayrshire, Haley House, on the periphery of Largs. We loved to visit her and I'd look out of her room's window and see the Isle of Cumbrae. We sometimes took Gran to Nardini's cafe where we scoffed their wonderful ice-cream or Knickerbockers' Glory. Those were happy outings. I wondered if she had gone to Largs.

Later that night mother returned with a calm, untroubled look on her face. She informed us that she had to visit her mother that day. She arrived and went to her room. Gran smiled at her only child. They spoke little but Mum held her hand and Gran closed her eyes, never to open them.

She explained her sudden departure quite simply. She had heard her mother call her in a dream the previous night and she knew she had to visit her the very next morning.

Dr Debra Drown is a Vermont resident and a New Hampshire clinical psychologist. She is a true friend, who with her husband Larry has visited us in Scotland on several occasions. Sadly Dr Larry Bart, her husband, also a clinical psychologist, suffered from Alzheimer's syndrome and was in a Care Home. However he died of Covid 19 in the autumn of 2020. This is Debra's subsequent dream.

A widow's dream

Last night I did dream that Larry was coming home and I couldn't find a wheelchair. I was puzzled and worried. That's all, just a fragment, other fragments of colours and an obnoxious man, I recall.

I hope you and yours are safe and warm this Christmas. Such a dark Covid 19 time.

Another dream

So my waking dream this morning was of little electric purple wasps. A cloud flying around. I'm wondering if that's my internal representation of the virus. Don't know. But I did wake up with the song 'Purple Rain' by Jimmy Hendrix **playing in my subconscious. I swear, my brain is a jukebox. Who knows how these things are connected in there?**

Love
Debra

Chrys Salt MBE has performed across the UK, Europe, India, Australia and the Yukon. She was International Poet at The Tasmanian Poetry Festival last year (2019). She has been the recipient of awards and bursaries (various): and was awarded an MBE in the Queen's Birthday Honours List for Services to The Arts in 2014. Here, she presents two poems dedicated to those suffering from dementia.

ALZHEIMER'S WALTZ

They're doing the Alzheimer Waltz
the one two three Alzheimer Waltz
the tune is an oldie
beyond all recall
but they pivot and twirl
on a sixpence of dreams
his suit double breasted
her stockings with seams
all sense disconnected
unplugged from the wall
they're doing the Alzheimer Waltz
waltz of forgetfulness
danced in a wilderness
caught between
somewhere and been there before
they know all the steps
but can't think what they're for
in the
one two three
Alzheimer Waltz

They're doing the Alzheimer Waltz
the one two three Alzheimer Waltz
on snub slippered feet
that forget they remember
the dance tunes of spring-time
in dying December
they shimmy and swirl
light fantastic unerring
a dashing young soldier
a slip of a girl
in the
one two three
Alzheimer Waltz

They're doing The Alzheimer Waltz
the one two three Alzheimer Waltz
and the lights on the tree
are as bright as the light
in the eyes of the dancers
who take to the floor
in the one two three
one two three
one two three
one two three
one two three Alzheimer Waltz

Dreams of quiet loss

Not that she doesn't remember,
but moments of quick forgetting,
increasingly beset her
between rising and dressing,
wanting and getting.

Not finding pieces of the sky to fit
or knows the name for it.
Saying 'sky'
as if, triumphant, finds
a missing piece.
The picture on the lid eludes.

A shutting and opening
of slatted blinds
that words slip through
words she once
looked so good in
pile unlaundered
in corners of her mind.
Sometimes the face of someone dear
who is not who she thinks is near
although they smile.

When we have gone,
She asks a stranger
if they'll take her home.

The Fishing Net

Miller Caldwell

It was from Fraserburgh's harbour that the fishing boat left on the early evening of a summer day. I recall that fateful summer holiday which snuffed out the life of my stillborn sister. Sadness and bewilderment was layered on my mind. Boarding the fishing boat was escapism for me. I was the lone landlubber on the fishing boat – no minister was ever allowed onboard for superstitious reasons beyond my ken and so the fishing trip I was promised, was without parental attendance.

The dream started with a memorable mug of tea, drowned with condensed milk. Consequently it was served sweet but helped me to cope with the swaying motions of the vessel. It was nearing the third hour as the boat was heading for Lybster on the extreme north-north east coast of Scotland when light faded and the work of harvesting the sea began.

I was given a line with no bait. The green nylon line had sixteen hooks shaded by various colours of plastic strips. I did as I was instructed and stood at the edge of the boat having slipped my hooks overboard and let them drop to the seabed. As soon as I raised the line, I felt tugs. Mackerel had attached themselves to the hooks in great numbers. I struggled to bring some of them aboard.

Before any fisherman saw my difficulties and came to assist me, the mackerel, as if directed by a company major, turned away from the boat and I followed on, diving headlong into the choppy water. I had no time to shout and the boast's engine must have drowned the shock I expressed anyway as I entered the cold water. I felt a peaceful descent into the dark sea and realised after a few moments that I must have drowned. I floated and swam like a fish until a dolphin nudged me. It swam alongside me and I took hold of its dorsal fin. I kept my feet together, streamlining the dolphin's progress. It brought me to the seabed after a while and to a crevice in the rocks. It was about my bedtime so I slept secure in the knowledge that the dolphin had become my guard and hovered around until the day broke.

It seemed a short sleep but I could see the light of the sea surface above me when I woke. However, there was much to see on the seabed. A submarine lay quite nearby. I approached it. It had U507 on its turret. A WW2 victim.

The German submarine, still rusting while sunk in the sandy ground at such an angle it seemed to be giving a Nazi salute, seemed interesting. I swam over to it and, amid sharp eroding metal, I entered. I was not the first to do so. Many small fish were already in the submarine, making it a sanctuary from larger fish. They tickled me. There were no bodies to encounter, just bones. But an Enigma secret communication lay battered. A last minute attempt at destroying the German secret coding which unknown to them at the time was already in the hands of decoders at Bletchley Park lay before me. I left the submarine as it seemed too eerie for me.

Then a large squid approached with dancing tentacles. They wound round me like a Boa Constrictor snake. I gasped as the tentacles tightened around my body. Then a white shark swam close by and decided the squid was its meal. It attacked two of its tentacles and suddenly I was released as the squid fought for its survival. I patted the white shark on its back as I swum past.

I met King Neptune who was enthroned on his seaweed draped throne. His green clad regal chair was a boulder cut out to seat him as he held his trident before me. He asked me what I was doing and I told him, that I must have drowned. I had been on a fishing boat and fell over. He told me I was one of many fishermen who had drowned. He descended his throne and in a cave behind him, he invited me to enter.

There were many who turned their heads and smiled inanely. As they greeted me, I detected Cornish, Aberdonian, Yorkshire and Lancashire accents of smiling fishermen. I also detected the Hanseatic accents of north German sailors drinking beer with

British sailors. No longer enemies of the mid-century world conflict, they shared jokes. There were no arms or ammunition in sight but fraternal gestures abounded. I waved at them and turned around. King Neptune had gone and I swam away, with a wave to the drowned former foes, towards the light of daytime on land. As I broke the surface, I realised I was near the shore. A few rocks lined the shoreline and I swam to them. I climbed up one rugged boulder and took a gasp of air. I awoke.

My scientific badminton playing friend writes:

A Scientist's Dream

Recalling dreams is a tough one for me. Most of the time, if I have been dreaming, I have only very vague recollections.

I've been lucky to have a couple of lucid dreams with one of them in particular being very exciting as it involved me hurtling down a steep cobbled street on a bike. I knew I was dreaming but felt every bump with the wind blasting in my face.

I've also had a couple of times when I had a dream within a dream with a false awakening but the content escapes me which suggests they were quite boring.

I do, however, remember from the 80s dreaming of an answer to a logic problem as part of a microelectronics circuit board lesson. This was a new course which Fiona and Laura (the author's daughters) may remember. *It involved NOT, AND and OR* gates. A NOT gate turned an input of 1 into an output of 0 and vice-versa. To get an output of 1 from an AND gate, both inputs had to be at 1. For an output of 1 from an OR gate either input could be at 1. (Are you still awake, class?) The inputs came from light and heat sensors and also a switch. The outputs could go to a buzzer, lamp or external circuit. You were given problems to solve. E.g. if you want a buzzer to sound to warn you when your greenhouse was overheating but one you could switch off, you would attach the heat sensor and the switch to the AND gate and the output to the buzzer.

I think the problem that neither I nor the pupil who had got to it failed, was something to do with a buzzer warning of frosty conditions at night. That night I dreamt of connecting both the heat sensor and light sensor into an OR gate (so with two 0's going in the output would be 0) and then connect that output to a NOT gate which turned the 0 into a 1 which activated the buzzer. Looking back it all seems very simple.

Kekule's solution to the structure of benzene came though this dream.

Alan Collins Originally hailing from the former steel town of Motherwell, Alan spent 43 years with the Annan based boilermakers, Cochran &Co, rising to the position of Director of Export Sales. However before retiring in 2008, Alan took up a secondment in China to manage a Joint Venture Company which Cochran had formed along with a Shanghai pressure vessel manufacturer. Alan now lives in Lockerbie with his wife Muriel and has two sons Richard and Alastair, and a daughter Emma.

Electric Cars and the Everly Brothers and Revolution in the Air.

My goodness, responding to your question is quite a challenge because as you observe, as much as 95% of dreams are forgotten, which leads you to wonder what was so significant about the dreams of the remaining 5%? Or that they had such an impact on the subconscious part of their minds, that they can recollect the content of their dream? Or perhaps it was a subdued nightmare?

My own dreams strangely feature part of my working life which came to an end in January 2008, and do include a travel element and all the vagrancies which can happen, and for me at times they did, especially in Asia and the Middle East. The dream did not reflect what actually happened, but more a variation of a situation. My former colleagues also made cameo appearances. The details are of course lost, but the timing is usually before waking up in the morning.

Amusingly, recently I have tried to get myself to sleep by imagining how I could live with a battery powered car. Needless to say by the time I nodded off, I had no answer and on waking the same question was still floating around in my mind.

Dream feedback from my chums in the Lockerbie Probus Club.

One says that he would need to "clean them up" before relating them to anyone.

David, our Treasurer and a former teacher and school headmaster tells me that he dreams on a regular basis and again his teaching experiences appear to influence the subject matter of his dreams, whilst some of the characters he met when he and his wife lived in Hereford have recently featured in his dreams.

The work related influence seems to be a motivating factor for many of us as we wander through the dark hours of the night.

Incidentally - one of my favourite songs is 'All I have To Do is Dream' by the Everly Brothers. A great karaoke song by the way!

I was invited to give a talk to the membership of Lockerbie Rotary which I did last night by means of Zoom. I have to say that it went down well, at least the response was genuine, which was pleasing. My subject matter was REVOLUTIONS which included the Islamic Revolution of 1979 and the reason why we moved from Uddingston to Lockerbie, the Industrial Revolution, the Digital Revolution and finally the new Workplace Revolution which is now upon us. Presenting like this is certainly the way forward whether because of Covid 19 or otherwise.

Stuart Clark, is an Edinburgh resident and water engineer who dreams regularly. His friend Fiona is mentioned in this contribution. His dream starts off with a truism. Yes, have a notepad ready by your bedside.

The Mediaeval Swordsman

Hi Miller,

So it turns out I can vividly remember my dreams for about five minutes after I wake up so I really need to keep a notepad next to the bed.

So last night/this morning, I dreamt that there were monsters around Edinburgh and that I had to show Fiona how to protect herself. Now the only thing I had (for whatever reason) was a small sgian-dubh so I was trying to best show her how to use it. Then as dreams go, they morphed into me wielding a broadsword in one hand and a dirk in another, Jacobean style, cleaving away with the broadsword in one hand and raking with the dirk in the other, down a city street with an assortment of monsters. Some were even flying whilst I was shouting at Fiona to follow me!

My other dream involved buying a car with my 'mates' one of whom was the American actor Shia LaBeouf (he was in *Fury* and I had to Google his name.) The other one was someone else famous but I cannot remember who. I must write these things down for you.

A Game of Football

Miller Caldwell

I found myself dreaming of playing football. My brother was in the team. I was the goal keeper saving crosses, shots and prospective high punts. The goalie, of course, is the last line of defence. I came with the ball to the edge of the penalty area and threw the ball to my brother, Bruce. He was on the wing and like a dancing nymph he wove his way goal wards. The other goalkeeper advanced and as he was a few feet away, Bruce chipped the ball over him and the ball trickled into the empty net. It was the only goal of the game. I ran to celebrate his goal at the halfway line and gave him a strong cuddle. I could not let him go. I held on to him until I woke.

My brother, Bruce, died four years before this dream.

Catherine Czerkawska is a well-known Scottish author who has provided an interesting dream about fact. She is a novelist, historian and experienced professional playwright, living in rural south Ayrshire.

New York 11th September

OK – here's my dream. Nightmare really and a bit spooky, writes author Catherine.

The night before 11th September 2001, I had one of the most appalling nightmares I've ever had.

I was in the middle of some catastrophe and was trying to escape. People were screaming, and dust and chunks of masonry were raining down from the sky.

I remember running and trying to take shelter from it all, underneath some kind of structure that we thought might protect us. Anything to get away from whatever was falling.

I woke up in a cold sweat - it was such a horrible dream that I told my husband, Alan, about it. It stayed with me all morning, and coloured my day, the way dreams like that do.

Then, in the afternoon, a friend phoned us and said 'switch on your television. There's something happening at the twin towers....'

If I hadn't told Alan about it, I don't think anyone would have believed me – but he will vouch for what I told him. It gave him such a frisson too.

Later on, I believe, some research was done - and many people seem to have had similar dreams - more than could be accounted for by 'coincidence'.

It was such a graphic and particular dream, as well, with nothing to account for it. I hadn't been watching any disaster movies or anything like that!

Hugh McMillan is a poet from Penpont in South West Scotland. His work has been published widely in Scotland and beyond, and he has won various prizes, most recently the Callum Macdonald Memorial Award in 2017 for *Sheep Penned*, published by Roncadora; he won the same award in 2009 for *Postcards from the Hedge*.

Not Actually Being in Dumfries: New and Selected poems was published by Luath Press in 2015 as were in 2018 the poetry collections *Heliopolis*, and *The Conversation of Sheep*, the latter in collaboration with a local shepherd. He has featured in many anthologies, and three times in the Scottish Poetry Library's online selection *Best Scottish Poems* of the year. His poems have also been chosen three times to feature on National Poetry Day postcards, the latest in 2016. In 2017 he was writer in residence at the Harvard Summer School. In 2020 he was chosen as one of 4 'Poetry Champions' for Scotland, to seek out and commission new work.

His website is at https://www.hughmcmillanwriter.co.uk/

Dream

Midnight and phone dead,
the Innocent Tunnel is a wormhole,
the walls slick and vivid.
I am in Scotland like some vein:
up there all the weans are quiet
and the streets are gaunt and rain
washed and the poets are scheming
and the politicians are sound asleep.

The paths sprout like capillaries.
I take the one that leads to sages,
Tim Propp, Robert Louis Stevenson,
Big Mary of the Songs.
They are talking silently:
there are ruins but no culture, they say,
there is hatred but no criticism.
there are crowds but no community.
Where are our people, the bard asks.
Despite all our most fervent
tweeting we are not saving the world
not even this small part Scotland,
land of glaur and thrawn misery
where the people feast on each other.
We stare at the gas lamps which make
a gauze like glow and the umbers deep
in the well of the bar where we are reflected
over and over again with that beard
or shawl or bicycle receding to infinity.
We sit in mid century silence and
our thoughts turn to those who occupy
our heads like a sullen army. We raise
our tall shining glasses to the dead,
to the list that is unending, to the faces.
I hear my daughter playing a lament:
she has been practising for years
and is now good enough to break my heart.
The tunnel is narrowing into a point
of throat like the foam and then the rest
of a pint might, like being unborn back
into the depths of the atomic soul.
Day will cover the city like a fire blanket.

Not often do we dream in vivid colour. The colour Red, accordingly, does not feature regularly in dreams. **Alan Collins** sheds light on 'Seeing Red' in its many disguises.

Seeing Red

Alan Collins

Many of us can probably recall, describing to a friend, a situation or event which makes you angry as a result of something which was said or done to such an extent that your reaction could only be described as **"seeing red"**. The choice of the colour red in this expression is of course a reference to the traditional belief that the colour red makes bulls angry in bullfighting. Remember the matador waves a red cape to make the bull charge. For the writer, to be **seeing red** has not always been in the context of anger or aggression, although it has, but has been used to describe why at the time, the colour red was important and meaningful.

My first example which comes into the category of **"seeing red"** relates to one of motoring's most persistent myths – the waving of a Red Flag in front of a moving vehicle. It is still widely believed that the London to Brighton Veteran Car Rally is the longest running motoring event in the world, first run in 1898 and called "The Emancipation Run". It celebrated the then recently passed Locomotives on Highways Act of 1898, which liberalised motor vehicle laws and which dropped the need for a red flag to be waved in front of a moving vehicle.

The red flag requirement first began with the Locomotive Act of 1865 (the Red Flag Act) which required all road locomotives, which included automobiles, to travel at a maximum speed of 4 mph in the country and 2 mph in the city, as well as requiring a man carrying a red flag to walk as much as 60 yards in front of road vehicles hauling multiple wagons. The purpose being to warn pedestrians of the approach of this potentially dangerous horseless carriage or wagon.

The legislation was, of course, initially designed for the traction engines which then travelled our roads before the arrival of the motor car. However, in 1878, an amendment to this Act came into force which reduced the red flag distance to just 20 yards. The subsequent 1896 Act removed from the 1865 Act, certain restrictions including the need for a red flag, raising the speed limit to 14 mph. It provided legislation that allowed the automotive industry in the United Kingdom to develop soon after the emergence of the first practical motor car, an event which is commemorated each year when the owners and their passengers dress in period clothes. Exposed to the elements, they attempt to drive their cherished motor cars 64 miles from Hyde Park in London to the promenade in Brighton.

Still on a motoring theme, and my first personal example of me **"seeing red"** was when in 1965 I was finally in a position to buy my first real car, a Mini, an Austin Seven actually as the Austin version was called, and it had to be in Tartan Red just like the BMC Works rally cars. Like many I was captivated by the Mini, as prior to the introduction of this fabulous little roller skate of a car the Austin A35 and the Morris Minor (also designed by Alex Issigonis) were the two most popular small family cars on the market. Both however appeared antiquated and without character, whereas this new Mini was a breakthrough in packaging, handling, and of course, it had character in spades, it was classless had a smiley face and was simply fun on wheels. I often dreamt about this car.

The Mini was first introduced to the motoring world in October 1959, (I still have my copy of the *Autocar* magazine which was full of sepia and black and white pictures, cut away drawings and the all-important road test of the car). I was just 15 at the time, living with my parents in Motherwell, and as I was so captivated by the concept of this tiny miracle of a car,

I would regularly cycle up to Taggart's Austin showroom to gaze in awe at this little wonder sitting on 10" wheels. Each time I went there I would collect another brochure which I would read from cover to cover. Sad to admit that I even slept with a copy placed under my pillow, and dreamt, and so my ambition from that moment onwards was to be in a position one day to buy one, and it had to be the Austin version. And yes, it had to be in Tartan Red, and not the cherry red of its Morris twin. Turning 18 and with a new driving licence in my pocket, and to keep up with my pals, my means of transport was an unreliable red 1937 MG TA. However, despite it eventually suffering from a cracked cylinder head, and having originally bought the car for the princely sum of £85, a buyer was found paying me £55 before towing it away. And so, after this unsuccessful experience, I was then determined that my next wheels just had to be a Mini, so aged 21 and on completion of my apprenticeship as draughtsman with a boiler making company, I found a new job also in a boiler drawing office. With plenty of overtime available, serious saving began, and as a result, within six months I had saved enough money to put down a healthy deposit, and to be able to proudly walk into Taggart's showroom in April 1965 to place my order for a Tartan Red Mini Super De Luxe. A few weeks later I was a proud owner of my first new car which bore the registration DGM 299C, and all for a total on the road price of £555. That day, as I excitedly drove home to show my parents my new pride and joy, I was truly **"seeing red"** but it was a very happy red.

In 1998 I received from my MD a gift which came in the form of a Red Letter day the subject of which was an invitation to participate in a Ferrari driving Experience which was held at the Mallory Park racing circuit in Leicestershire, and which involved me driving two Ferraris. First was a V8 followed by a V12, and both in the famous Ferrari red, around the Leicestershire circuit. After a brief drive around the circuit with an instructor in a VW Golf during which he pointed out the braking points and the suggested "racing line", I was then provided with a protective suit and a crash helmet and introduced to my first Ferrari, a V8 Mondial. I was allowed only three laps, and despite the presence of the instructor beside me, and scoring all aspects of my driving, I thought that I had acquitted myself quite well.

We then returned to the pits where my next charge, a V12 Testa Rossa awaited, and again only three laps were allowed, but my confidence was such that I was able to adopt a better line through the corners whilst braking deeper into the corners and negotiating the "esses" with hardly any reduction in speed. With so much power available, there was no need to explore the gears above third.

On completion, and with all the other would-be racing drivers present, the score cards were handed out and I was delighted to see that I had been awarded a score of 147 out of 150, and with the instructor's summary as follows.

"A good style developing with each lap, top marks for concentration."

I was truly **"seeing red"** that day, but it was the deep red of two Ferraris.

In a slightly different context, but still on a motoring theme, in 2019 I was again **"seeing red"**, but it was an angry red, when I discovered that my wife had hit a pothole in Dumfries, with the result that the car's two nearside tyres suffered split sidewalls. However, being run-flats, we were able to drive the car the short distance to my oldest son's house in Dumfries. A quick call to my youngest son, who thankfully was in the motor trade at the time, was able to organise a car transporter to take the car to his work where he had located replacement tyres of the same spec and brand. Having hit a pothole hard, there was also a need to check tracking and any other damage. Luckily later that day I was able to collect the car along with a hefty bill for all the work done. Despite my **"seeing red"** annoyance over this incident, and because we could not be 100% sure of the actual pothole which did the damage, and as the success rate for such claims on local authorities was not high, I had been prepared to write off the experience. However, my son and a friend insisted that I should submit a claim to the Dumfries & Galloway Regional Council to recover the cost of two tyres, transporting the car to the tyre shop and checking tracking etc. Despite the uncertainty as to the identity of the guilty pothole, and the profusion of potholes which exist within the town's boundaries, by a process of elimination, we found what we were pretty sure was the correct pothole a relatively short distance from my son's house, and so a claim form with photographic evidence along with invoices was submitted to the department concerned. An acknowledgement along with a few questions was received from the Council's insurers, to which I responded, and to my delight several weeks later an offer of compensation was received.

However, my initial delight was transformed to that of **"seeing red"**, when I read that the insurers were reducing my claim because of depreciation and the high mileage of the car. I challenged their reasoning for reducing the value of my claim as the mileage of the car had nothing to do with split side walls. In two years, I had only done 14,000 miles and as I could only replace the tyres with new ones, their argument was not logical. In the end they relented and offered me a much more acceptable settlement which I accepted. Lesson learned, avoid potholes, and adopt a Mr Grumpy attitude by challenging all that is unfair or unjust, because you might simply be proved correct and secure a positive outcome.

My next example of **"seeing red"** was when in 2005 I accepted a position to be General Manager of a new Sales and Marketing company in Shanghai, China. This was part of a joint venture my old company Cochran Boilers entered into with a local pressure vessel manufacturer to produce Cochran industrial boiler products in the PRC.

As you are aware, the Chinese Red Flag, the national flag of the Peoples Republic of China, is predominantly red, and is by tradition, or perhaps decree, flown prominently from all buildings of prominence in the vast country. This included the two flagpoles positioned at the entrance to my apartment building in Shanghai and as a result, could not be avoided, so first thing each morning, and at the end of the working day, I was **"seeing red"** in the form of the national flag of the PRC fluttering in the breeze.

Going out there on my own was a wonderful, perhaps slightly selfish, experience, as it left my wife at home, and with my mother not in the best of health in Motherwell, Muriel had to visit her each week. This proved unfortunate. It was a stressful experience for her, so when my period of secondment eventually ended, it was certainly time to return home. I was however returning to the UK three times each year, and of course, I phoned home on an almost daily basis.

When I first went out there I was also just three years short of retirement, having planned to retire on reaching 64, so I took the view that a one year secondment would be an ideal way of preparing to retire. However, such was the level of work involved, a second year was added, and once that was over I returned on the 19th December 2007 and into retirement on the 7th Jan 2008 when I did reach 64.

I was already familiar with China having flown in and out on regular sales visits since 1994. However, I had always harboured a notion to actually live and work in a different culture and not just visit for a few days at a time, so when asked, I requested the weekend to decide. However, knowing that an invitation was likely, I had already made up my mind, and truthfully there was no one else in the company qualified for the role. So, following a discussion with Muriel, I indicated my willingness to take on the role and to develop our business in China.

The reality is that China, a relatively safe country for ex patriots, especially in Shanghai where in those days it was believed that there were more than 300,000 living and working in this expanding and exciting city, a city which in so many ways resembled almost any large city in the Far East. And with Western influences everywhere, it was an easy place in which to be based. As a result, over two years I experienced both the joy and the stress of living and working in this fast developing country. The joy was of course in dealing with the Chinese people, both those well used to dealing with westerners, and those in the more remote regions who were more curious, but always prepared to demonstrate their hospitality and to make me welcome. Travelling throughout this huge and diverse country with its 31 provinces, each almost a country on its own, and with its own culture and populations measured in the millions, was a fantastic experience, and one for which I will always be grateful.

My first year in position was very encouraging, with much success securing contracts for both imported and locally manufactured products. However, the reason for my **"seeing red"** moments was the eventual failings of our Joint Venture partner, who was pursuing an entirely separate agenda, and one which created huge difficulties for me, and my client relationships. As a result, soon after I completed my two year secondment in December 2007, the JV sadly followed the path of many other similar JV's and was disbanded. I was very disappointed that after such a huge effort it ended this way. I am however pleased to say that Cochran are still active in the PRC but under a new structure which importantly, they control.

Memorable experiences for me were securing a huge contract for the supply of Annan built boiler plant for the new Shanghai Pudong International Airport which was at the time under construction, and also winning the contract to supply Annan manufactured boilers for the Great Hall of the People in Beijing. This gave me the opportunity to be given a private tour of the People's Great Hall.

However, one of the down sides of China business and one which annoyed me intensely, and yes, had me **"seeing red"** on many an occasion, was when I had a need to visit a number of potential suppliers of combustion equipment, pumps, valves and other fittings. They proudly showed me their products. But much of what they had on offer was recognisable and copied from well-known British and European Original Equipment Manufacturers. The lack of respect by the Chinese of intellectual property rights is well known. However, such are the advances of technology in China; there is now less need to copy the products of foreign companies. Nevertheless, at times it did make me **"see red"**!

> **Jess Bart** is the Chinese adopted daughter of Dr Debra
> Drown and the late Dr Larry Bart of Vermont.

> The context for this dream is that Jess and her mother
> recently watched *One Child Nation*, a documentary about
> Chinese girl children and adoption trafficking. That was
> quite disturbing.

Dreaming in China – One Child Nation

Jess dreamed she was on an excursion to China with her best friends from elementary school. They went into a CVS (American drugstore, this wouldn't be in China - a Chemist's shop in Britain). There was a beautiful white puppy for sale, at $8.95. Jess's friends wanted her to buy it, but she thought back and forth about how to take care of a puppy when they were all going to be sightseeing. She asked the drugstore people to take care of it. She also debated about the fact that the puppy was going to grow up to be a big standard poodle and she didn't want a standard poodle. But she didn't want the puppy to die. So she left it with the drugstore people, thinking she would return and decide about the puppy hoping it would still be alive. In the documentary that Jess and Debra watched, little girl babies were being left to die by the side of the road. When international adoption began, traffickers began to pick them up and sell them to orphanages.

> *'Happiness is not easily won; it is hard to find it in ourselves and*
> *impossible to find it elsewhere.'*
> NICOLAS CHAMFORT

Carlo, Mole and the Search for Happiness

Words and illustrations by Christina Scholz

It began among the long reeds and the lily pads at the water's edge. A whisper of mist rose from the banks of the fishpond in the gentle morning sun when all in the garden was still. No twittering of birds, no gentle hum of the bees; not a sound was to be heard through the silence. Somewhere a dew drop occasionally grew bold enough to roll down, and tickle awake those who had made themselves snug between the leaves and blades of grass. One such creature was Carlo, the little frog. A drop of dew splashed right against the back of his neck.

"Brrr… that's chilly," he murmured, shaking himself awake and stealing a glance up at the blue sky above. The morning was his favourite time and the thought of what each new day might hold brought a happy shiver of excitement to his tummy. Every day a new start! Brilliant!

Carlo loved his life at the pond and in his garden. But to be honest it wasn't exactly *his* garden. The extensive lawns, the fruit trees, the green privet hedges and the lush flowerbeds were, to be fair, home to many other inhabitants too.

Yet his were the shallow waters of the immediate bank. That was the small kingdom he had conquered and it offered everything a frog could need: clear water, abundant food and, above all, giant lily pads to hang out on all day. For some, it might have seemed a tedious existence. But not for Carlo. As the sun shone warmly on his belly and the soft lily pads swayed gently on the water he would daydream. In his mind he would travel to distant wondrous gardens. These held new mysteries and secrets to explore every day. And that kept his mind occupied as he lay upon his favourite lily pad, wiling away the hours dreaming of wonderful adventures. It was an exciting pastime. It was in this way that Carlo felt he travelled far and wide to distant lands, from which he always returned the hero.

Indeed, his life seemed so full of dreamy adventures that he felt obliged to share his exciting travels with others. And it had become his habit to entertain his neighbours by relating his magnificent stories to them every evening.

At first he held the inhabitants of the garden spellbound with captivating tales of high adventure. But, after a while, Carlo began to repeat the same stories and his audience began to drift away. They started to get bored. They'd heard it all before. In fact many of his neighbours began to actively avoid the little frog and suddenly became 'busy' doing other things. Only one listener remained loyal to Carlo and that was his friend Mole.

Part of the reason was that the storytelling took place at a time when Mole was just waking up and he had nothing particular to do as his senses adjusted from sleep to consciousness. But he genuinely treasured the stories told by the little frog. Similarities in the stories didn't bother him at all. Quite the contrary: the expectation of a familiar ending was wonderfully reassuring. In fact he was often able to whisper the exact words along with Carlo as the little frog related his adventure, which made the story even more vivid to him. Day and night, as he burrowed endless underground tunnels and passageways he was able to think about the wonderful experiences his friend described and forget his loneliness.

An evening like no other

And so it was that Carlo and Mole became the best of friends. They could hardly wait to see each other every evening. Their daily meeting always started the same way. Carlo would greet his friend with a cheerful "Good evening, Mole!" And then he would ask: "Do you know where I have travelled today?"

"No my dear friend," Mole would answer, before adding: "But I can't wait to find out!"

Yet today everything was different. Without any of the usual formalities, Carlo's story began to gush from him. He was coming to a particularly exciting and heroic part of the story when he suddenly caught the sadness and distance in his friend's eyes.

"What's the matter with you," he asked Mole, who seemed to be staring absently into space. "Are you even listening to me?"

"Please forgive me," his friend stammered, suddenly wrenched from his own distant thoughts. "Where were we with your story? Why don't you start again from the beginning? I'm sure it is another wonderful adventure." And he smiled encouragingly.

"Mole, my dear friend…" Carlo answered with a look of concern. "I think you should be telling the story today of just what is troubling you. You look so very sad."

"Do you really think so?" said Mole. And he hesitated before continuing. "You know, Carlo, just lately I've been worried about a particular problem…"

"And it just won't go away?" asked Carlo thoughtfully. It was more of a statement.

"It does," said the mole, scratching the thick fur on his head. "But only if I manage to think of something even more terrible. It's now got to the stage that my brooding led me to tunnel so deep underground that in the end I didn't know what was above and what was below. Thankfully a big tree root managed to show me the way back to the surface." Mole sighed.

"My dear friend…" Carlo said with concern. "What is it that makes you so sad today?"

Mole looked thoroughly miserable and seemed to struggle under the weight of what he wanted to say.

"I… erm… I don't want to be a mole anymore," he suddenly exclaimed. "I don't want to live underground, missing every day. There are so many things in this garden I have never seen in daylight…"

"But Mole, don't I describe everything to you from my travels to beautiful distant places?" Carlo was trying to comfort his friend, who was looking increasingly tearful and distressed.

"But that's exactly what the problem is! I can't even dream my own adventures. And do you know why that is?"

Carlo shrugged his shoulders. He wasn't sure.

"Because I'm a mole! And moles live out their lives in the dark and can't see anything. And if you can't see things, then you can't even begin to dream about them!"

"Ah, now I understand," Carlo said uncertainly, for he still wasn't sure.

"What I wouldn't give to be a bird and to travel across the world and see the beauty of different places. Then I would be able to dream just like you," said the mole. Then he sighed deeply and sadly, and began to tunnel back into the ground, leaving Carlo to puzzle exactly what it must be to be a mole.

Courage for a friend

The next day, as the sun began to sink below the far side of the pond, Carlo went to visit his friend as usual. But having arrived at the entrance to Mole's underground home he waited and waited. But Mole did not appear. The same thing happened the next evening and the evening after. Carlo's friend was not to be seen. And the little frog began to worry and blame himself.

"How could I have made Mole so unhappy with my stories? What if he is so deep and lost in thought again that he can't find his way back to the surface?" Carlo dared not think any more about what might have happened to his friend. He decided it was a time for action!

And so the little frog began to ask every creature and every living thing in the garden about his friend. First he spoke to the whispering grass. But it was silent. Next he asked the fruit trees whether any had felt Mole brush past their roots. Yet they gave no clue. Nor was there an answer from the privet hedges. He tried the sunflowers too. Yet they simply hung their heavy heads.

A sense of panic began to grow within the little frog. Who else could he ask? The garden seemed strangely empty on this of all days. Neither beetles, or fellow frogs, rabbits or mice were to be seen far and wide.

But then he spotted a strange large bird standing motionless among the rushes on the far side of the pond, as if made of stone.

"Perhaps the bird has seen my friend," Carlo thought. Yet to ask the bird the question he would have to cross the length of the entire pond. Of course, in theory that would not be too difficult for a frog like Carlo. After all, he could simply jump from lily pad to lily pad. But he hesitated. Because there was the thought which seemed to hold him back like invisible giant hands taking hold of his shoulders. It was the fear he felt of the opposite bank. In his entire frog's life he had never crossed to the other side of the pond. And he was frightened.

Sure, in his dreams he'd had many adventures beyond his own familiar world. But now that the idea of leaving everything he knew presented itself, he could think of nothing more appealing than lying comfortably and safely upon his favourite lily pad in the sun.

"What a cowardly frog I am," he told himself. "My dear friend Mole is in difficulty and I am scared to even cross the pond. I'm his only friend. Therefore I am the only one who can help him."

Carlo decided he must push his fear away. And to prove his courage to himself he decided to make his first leaps the biggest, longest, most masterful frog jumps ever!

Arriving at the other side of the pond he almost froze as he found himself staring up at the strange bird, which had looked much smaller from the other side of the pond. Now, though, the magnificent creature's long and spindly legs seemed to stretch endlessly upwards; its beak was enormous and extraordinarily threatening. Its plumage too seemed dark and menacing in the half-light of the approaching evening. And hadn't the older, wiser frogs always warned against large, threatening birds? No matter! He simply had to find his friend, whether it was dangerous, or not. Again, Carlo had to gather all his courage and speak to the large bird.

"Mr. Strange and Magnificent Bird… I don't want to disturb you, but have you seen my dear friend Mole?"

But the bird did not answer. It continued to stand still and silent. It was only when Carlo repeated his question in his loudest voice that the magnificent creature before him slowly turned his head and gazed down at him regally along an enormous beak.

"If you continue to disturb me I am not likely to catch another fish today," said the bird slowly, with a hint of irritation.

"I'm sorry Mr. Magnificent Bird," Carlo answered, surprised by the courage in his own voice. "But I am so worried about my friend. I've looked everywhere for him. And I've crossed from the other side of the pond in the hope that you might perhaps…"

"I don't think so," said the bird dismissively. "I'm not from here. Just travelling through. Apart from you I haven't seen anyone. Besides, I'm very tired and very hungry and don't have time for missing moles!"

Carlo's shoulders dropped, his head hung low, as if he was carrying the weight of many sorrows. He could no longer hide his disappointment, his fear and his sadness from the strange bird, which continued to stare down at him. And big tears began to roll down the little frog's face, which was usually so happy.

The crane was startled, for the majestic bird had never ever seen a frog cry before in all his many years of travel.

"I think I must apologize for my rudeness," the crane stammered, much moved by Carlo's sorrow. And the bird bowed low towards Carlo to gaze into the little creature's eyes, turning his head sideways, so that his giant beak was not in his way.

"Please sit with me and tell me all about your worries," said the crane. "I'm sure a fish will find its way to me in good time," the bird added, nudging the little frog's shoulder tenderly with his beak. So Carlo began to tell the crane all about his absent friend, their usual meetings and the plan Mole had shared with him to leave his underground world to follow his dream and find happiness.

Happiness is a rare bird

The crane listened carefully to Carlo's story before speaking with the wisdom and experience of the well-travelled.

"Well, my little friend, it's strange and elusive, this thing called happiness. We are all looking for it. But not everyone is able to find it. You have to believe in it. But above all, you have to look for it in the right places."

"But what is the right place?" Carlo wanted to know.

"Take it easy. Slowly, slowly, my friend. That's not so easy to answer. But perhaps I can explain things better if you knew who I am. Which reminds me, I haven't introduced myself, have I?"

Carlo stared at the bird with a sense of expectation. But before he revealed who he was the crane puffed up his plumage majestically. Then he raised his long, elegant neck with an extraordinary sense of importance, cleared his throat and announced: "I am a crane, a traveller, a messenger of good fortune and happiness."

"You're a messenger of happiness?" Carlo repeated doubtfully. "I've never heard of such birds."

Deflated by the little frog's response the crane's plumage shrank back against his body and he lowered his head.

"You really don't know what a crane represents?"

Carlo shook his head, a little confused. "No."

"Then I'd better explain," said the crane patiently, who had now recovered his composure. "We cranes are migratory birds, which means we are constantly on the move from place to place. In the autumn we fly great distances from north to south and in the spring we head back. But no matter where and when we arrive, people are always pleased to see us. We cranes are therefore known as carrying happiness on our wings."

"Really…" said Carlo uncertainly, for he still remembered the fear with which he had first laid eyes on the giant bird.

"Why are people so pleased to see you?" asked the little frog.

"Well…erm…" answered the crane slightly embarrassed. "To be honest and to be exact, we can't really take full credit for the happiness people feel. At the same time, that's our biggest secret."

"Oh wow…" said Carlo and began hopping excitedly around the crane. "Please tell me why you bring happiness then and what your secret really is?"

"It's all about…" The giant bird hesitated and gazed searchingly at the little creature before him. "Before I reveal the mystery you must promise to keep the secret. The other cranes might otherwise disown me. Carlo nodded in agreement and the crane began to explain.

"It is really because we cranes don't like the cold and the snow. We only feel comfortable in the warmth of the sun. Therefore our wings always carry us to places that will soon be warm and where new life is about to awake. Do you understand?" the crane asked the little frog.

"I'm not sure," answered Carlo.

"Wherever we land, spring is never far behind us. That's for sure. Everyone knows that. Well, almost everyone," added the crane with a chuckle.

"Aha! Now I understand," said Carlo with a sense of triumph. "Then it's not really the sight of you that makes people so happy. It's the thought that soon there will be warm sunshine, fresh growth and fragrant flowers!"

"That's right, my friend. But now I have said enough. Let us sleep, as it is very late now and tomorrow we have a busy day. After all, we don't yet have a plan to find your friend Mole," said the crane and offered to allow Carlo a place to sleep under his wing. The little frog nodded in agreement and snuggled into the softness of the crane's feathers. But before he fell asleep there was one thought that kept running through his mind: hope and the anticipation of good things ahead can bring a sense of happiness, he thought!

"I absolutely must tell Mole," he murmured as he fell into a deep and satisfying sleep.

Up and away

The crane awoke before the very first ray of sun had broken across the horizon, stretched his long legs, raised his elegant neck and offered a loud and hearty cry to welcome the new day, shaking Carlo from his sleep. Though the little frog loved the mornings, this was just a little bit too early – and he closed his eyes determined to doze and dream a little longer.

But the crane was resolute. "How on earth do you expect to find your friend Mole if you sleep through the whole morning?" said the bird sternly. "Besides, you have to welcome each and every morning with a cheerful 'hello' as you would a dear friend. Treat the morning with respect and a good day is sure to follow." Carlo watched the crane through sleepy eyes.

"You should follow my example," the bird continued. "I too have worries. I feel a sense of fear before every flight: will I manage to join my flock; will I take a wrong turn and arrive at the wrong destination? But once I am on my way my worries disappear and the journey turns out to be the best and most wonderful experience…"

The crane was in full swing, lecturing Carlo about the advantage of action, rather than worry. He was so impressed with his own words that he hadn't noticed the little frog had closed his ears and his eyes and was fast asleep once more.

"It's your turn now," said the crane, standing over Carlo. He grabbed the frog and shook him awake.

"What… what… what is happening?" cried Carlo in confusion, as he was shaken from his comfortable sleep.

"I said, it's your turn now. Come on!" insisted the bird.

"What do you mean?" Carlo didn't understand.

"You have to greet the new day," said the crane. "Doesn't matter how. Just as you please. Come on!" he insisted.

"If you think it is important for a frog, then I'll do it. But let me think," added Carlo, scratching his head. "Ah, I think I've got it," he said finally. "Good morning, lovely day!" he added sleepily.

The crane looked at him, unimpressed. "Is that it? With a little more *feeling*, please!"

"OK! I'll try it again," said Carlo closing his eyes tightly and trying to think. And as he thought of his friend Mole, the words seemed to flow naturally from him. "I've crossed the pond, I've met and spoken to the magnificent crane! And today I will be brave and fearless again for my dear friend."

It wasn't just the crane who was impressed. Carlo was himself surprised by the effect his own words had on him. It started with butterflies in the tummy, then a tingling from his toes to his fingertips, as if he was supercharged. The feeling was impossible to resist – and he suddenly smiled from ear to ear!

"Wow! What a feeling! Today I know I'm going to find Mole!" he said.

Visibly pleased, the crane tapped Carlo on the shoulder and pushed him gently towards the pond.

"As I missed out on my evening meal yesterday, I could do with a hearty breakfast to help me think. Unfortunately, we don't yet have any kind of plan about how to find your friend Mole," said the bird.

"But we do," Carlo said excitedly. "I've just remembered."

"Then let me hear it. You've made me curious," said the crane eagerly.

"Actually, it's quite simple. Mole said himself where we should look for him: not underground but up there, where the birds are. That's where he wanted to be! That was his plan."

"So how do you suggest we proceed?" asked the crane, scratching his head thoughtfully.

"Crane, you're the bird here. Surely you could carry me on your back and fly."

"Gosh! You're right," said the crane. "How stupid of me. Of course! Then let us set out at once. I will show you how a majestic crane flies."

No sooner said than done. With a single leap Carlo was upon the crane's back, who spread his mighty wings wide. Taking a short run-up, a powerful beat of his wings lifted them from the ground into the air.

Up and up they soared until the lake, its shoreline, the flowerbeds and the trees were no more than a tiny patchwork of colours on the ground far below. And everything familiar in Carlo's world now seemed strange and new seen from the sky.

In fact, Carlo couldn't seem to get enough of the new sensation he was experiencing. And he would have been happy to continue as they were forever in dreamlike wonder, had the crane not suddenly called out: "Mole spotted ahead!"

Indeed, there was Mole. Dead ahead. A little black ball of fluff clambering among the highest branches of a mighty fir tree. It was none other than Carlo's dearest friend, buffeted in the strong wind as the tree swayed from side to side.

"Yes, yes, that's him; that's my friend, Mole! Thank goodness we have found him," cried Carlo excitedly and in his impatience pressed his heels into the back of the crane, as if he were wearing spurs. But the crane remained calm and circled the crown of the tree a few times to seek out a safe platform among the branches on which to land.

"Steady, my friend. Steady. It's stormy up here and I need to be sure the branches can hold us," he said as any responsible pilot might before finally lowering himself skillfully close to the tree's trunk. Yet they were close enough to almost touch Mole.

"We can't stay long," said the crane, as the branches bent precariously under their weight. "Rescue your friend as quickly as you can, so that we can take off as soon as possible," said the crane.

"Mole!" cried Carlo with a mixture of worry and relief. "What are you doing up here?"

The little mole seemed completely exhausted. But hearing his friend's voice seemed to lift him as he called back to Carlo triumphantly.

"Up here? Yes, I am right up here! Am I at the very top?"

"Yes, my dear friend, you are right at the top! You can't get any higher than this," replied Carlo a little anxiously, as the crane was already signalling he was ready for take-off.

"I'm at the very top! Wonderful! Beautifully clear air, Mole said excitedly and wanted to clap his front paws together in happiness, were he not clinging so desperately to the tree branch.

And then Carlo had reached him and put his slender green arms around his friend.

"We have to go," he said, as a gust of wind rocked the tree. And he slid his friend across onto the safety of the crane's back just as the branch beneath them began to give way. "Just in time! Hold tight, Mole. We're off," he cried, as the giant bird launched himself back into the air with is two passengers.

"Off where?" asked Mole a little anxiously.

"We're flying, Mole! Flying high above the ground. And it's beautiful!" cried Carlo, holding onto his friend as tightly as he could.

The giant crane swept gracefully through the air, undaunted by the wind that buffeted them and flew several wide circuits high above the garden. Out across fields and forests, streets and houses, even over a small mountain he soared, sailing elegantly on the wind.

And Carlo described everything to his friend the mole, who smiled as he imagined the wonderful sights below. Mole was absolutely still as he listened to his friend's voice and enjoyed the breeze against his face and the sensation of flying high above the ground as he had always dreamed.

Then, following a flight that seemed to last forever, the crane began to sweep gently towards the ground towards the garden to land. And they were back at the water's edge at the pond they knew so well.

A happy ending

That evening they sat long and silently, side-by-side. The sun had set and the mist began to rise over the pond. All three felt that this had been a day to remember! A day on which they had done exactly what they had always wanted. They had achieved something wonderful.

"My friends," said the crane, eventually breaking the silence. "I'm not sure about you, but I'm enormously hungry!"

"So are we," agreed the other two companions.

"Let's see what delicacies the garden has to offer at this late hour," Carlo suggested.

And after they had eaten heartily they fell into a happy and satisfied sleep.

Next morning, even before it was fully light, Crane and Mole were wrenched from their sleep by their enthusiastic friend.

"Good morning, my lovely garden! I, Carlo, am a lucky frog, because this is my home!"

No sooner had the little creature sounded his greeting than the crane rose up in all his majesty and issued his own welcome to shatter the morning stillness. "Good morning, beautiful day! I am a proud crane and have the best friends a bird could have in this world!"

The mole, which was not familiar with any morning rituals, wasn't sure about the behaviour of his friends at all. But then he too allowed his thoughts to run free and let go of those things that restricted moles.

"I so wanted to be as free as a bird. And yet I remain a mole. But I now feel the bravest and most travelled mole ever," he said. And the three friends laughed and hugged each other. But the crane looked a little awkward, because once more his giant beak was in the way!

But even as they embraced warmly, they were interrupted by the cries so familiar to the crane that sounded across the morning sky. The bird knew them well. He composed himself, shaking his wings, stretched his long, elegant neck and raised his giant beak to answer the distant calls of his fellow cranes with a loud cry.

"It's time to say farewell," said the bird. "The summer here has already seen many days. The birds of my species are ready for the long journey south and I will fly with them.

"But I will return, with the next spring. And if ever anything is certain it is the turning of the earth and the coming of spring again."

"I know," said Carlo. "And I will be overjoyed to see you again. Not just because the spring carries the warm sun on its heels, but because you, my dear friend Crane will return to bring happiness."

"Thank you, Carlo. That's the nicest thing anyone has ever said to me." And with that the crane stretched and flapped his giant wings, launching himself into the air.

Carlo and Mole watched their friend climb high into the blue sky and join the flock of cranes flying high above the garden and disappear into the distance.

For a while the two friends sat as the sun climbed higher over the pond.

"Shall we?" said Carlo to Mole, who nodded. They had a new story to tell all the fellow creatures of the garden. It was a tale of courage, of friendship, of flying and adventure in search of happiness. Now they knew where it is to be found. Do you?!

BOXING DAY 2006

Miller Caldwell

It was Christmas Eve and I was disturbed. I felt uncomfortable as I slept in bed. I got up twice in a dozed state and returned to bed. My wife asked if I was OK and I grunted my response. I had been sleepwalking. But before I awoke on Christmas day, I had dreamt that the house shook. I was sure the pictures on the walls were hanging at rakish angles. That the dining room table was on its side and the dog was trapped underneath it. The bed came crashing through from the first floor to the kitchen below and windows cracked and broke, shedding splinters of glass around the house. The dog's paws were bleeding but she licked out the shards and would not let me touch her.

My wife kissed me wishing me a Merry Christmas and I responded with my assertion that an earthquake had hit us in Dumfries. It was not the traffic noise of a lorry accident nearby but a real earthquake, I was sure of it.

I knew I had been dreaming. But I did recall my recollections so well I repeated them to my wife later that Christmas morning.

Around 10:30 am on Boxing Day I set off with our collie for his morning walk. I walked down the cycle path on a firm tarmacadam surface with houses on either side of me. I expected I might hear the shouts of excited children playing with the presents Santa left the previous day. However the screams were from adults as well. It seemed everyone was programmed to shout out simultaneously and I felt it a very surreal moment. Our collie dog was unsure too. He looked up at me several times, distracted from the scents which always preoccupied his elongated snout.

Twenty minutes later I returned home. I opened the door and my wife came to greet me with a worried look. That was an earthquake, she informed me.

Strangely, there was no experience of an earthquake on my dog walk but in houses all over Dumfries people had experienced an earthquake measuring 3.7 on the Richter scale on Boxing Day 2006 at 10:40 am. Not a spectacularly high rate on the world Richter score but one of the UK's highest.

A little over a year before, on October 8th 2005 an earthquake measuring 7.7 on the Richter scale erupted killing 75 thousand people and making as many homeless and injured. In reality, two months later in January 2006 I would find myself in the NWFP of the Islamic Republic of Pakistan as the camp manager of 24,500 homeless and injured people at Mansehra.

Sadly, that was not a dream. But my Christmas morning 2006 dream predicted an earthquake 24 hours before it happened. Our British earthquakes are usually minimal. However the movement of pictures on house walls must be signs of the earth's weak stability, or some force beyond our ken. Such dreams and resultant predictions are therefore not so unusual.

> **Nicola Sharp** from Cumbria was a child psychiatrist. After
> taking ill she became a writer. We are both members of the
> Society of Authors Disabled and Chronically ill branch.

The Wedding Cake

I dream that I am sitting around a dining table with a family, but not my family. The mother has made a very elaborate cake and she places it on the table. It is round, and decorated with white icing and very delicate wild flowers made of icing. It could be a wedding cake. It will have taken days to make and I expect us to eat it with cake forks, napkins and ceremony. However, the mother grabs a hunk of it with her hand and starts gorging on it. The other three family members follow suit. When it is my turn to take a piece, there is just a small ragged section left, and all the icing flowers have been taken. I take a piece with my hand but then realise that there are now two other people at the table, and there is very little left for them. I feel guilty about this.

Then the mother serves a wooden bowl which contains half-eaten rolls and crusts, with fish paste spread on them. It looks like the remains on people's plates at a café. I take the most complete piece of bread, but it has been toasted and burnt, and the fish paste is dried up and old.

I only eat it to be polite. I would normally have thrown it away. The rest of the family are eating it with great reverence, as if they value it more than the elaborate cake.

I had this dream during a period of time when I'd given up my job due to chronic health problems. I was struck by the reversal of values, the idea that you could invest time and energy into making something special but then gobble it up, yet value something that would normally be disregarded or thrown away. I think it helped me accept some of the changes in my life.

Rahim Karim is an international award winning poet
from Kyrgyzstan.

Today I Was Happy in a Dream

Today I was happy in a dream
I didn't want to wake up.
I wanted so much to tighten that happiness
After such sensual bad weather.

Today I was unhappy in a dream
And I was ready to die suddenly in him.
After such a heart attack,
After such a heart attack!

Today I was happy in a dream
Rustles came from outside.
I didn't want to wake up for anything
Still awake, but miserable.

I Had a Dream

I had such a wonderful dream:
I was lying in bed and dozing…
Where did the Pope come from?
He was in a cassock, he shone all over.

The headdress touched the grey clouds,
And an ash-coloured beard…
Bent over me, point blank,
I trembled with excitement.

And in a mouth-to-mouth position,
He breathed his warm breath into me.
I woke up from a cough here,
Dawn has come, a light period.

Who was he? Perhaps an angel
Oh, how can I understand his gesture?
Has the holy Archangel appeared?
Was it Solomon, God the messenger?
Where to go, who to ask?
Will divination help me?
Why should you leave your dream now?
Fortunately?
Or litigation again?

Dunstan Written in a Dream

Or maybe all that was, was a dream
Or the dark delirium of one who has gone mad.
Or maybe it is the meaning of days gone by
Or the future, or Dunstan
Great poet…

Barely the baby opened for the first time
His eyes, as he immediately cried,
So proclaiming his arrival!
Blessed be that day
When you showed up… Hello honey
My fawn, little baby
Don't be afraid, everything is calm in this world
And the warpath has overgrown with the past…
Your hour has struck at the happiest time
Which cannot be burdened?

So we will live without getting used to death,
Keep all that exists in your soul.

So that everything around shimmers in song
The fire of love was awakening in us.
And you will glorify the day as you grow up
And he will remain entirely yours
With all its greatness and filth.

He wandered through life and hovered in dreams,
For a quarter of a century he sobbed in search:
Fought with flesh, reputed to be insane
A laughing stock for many doomed.
He stayed and wept endlessly,
Nobody saw his face.
The one who absorbed the whole world as eternity,
And he was aware of the transience of life.

But the hour struck, and he turned to stone,
And the ocean boiled underfoot,
When he parted with everything in the world,
Like a lonely sailboat swayed
Friends thought he was a fool –
Nobody knew such a language!
The space grew dim, the satellites fell behind,
But I saw him, others gave…
And his invisible goal burned,
And the grief of his beloved was,
And speech invaded the darkness of dreams,
When the soul was torn from defeat.

Since the voices have become deaf,
He was attracted to heavenly benevolence,
When he was burning with thirst in the desert
Suddenly as a bird ascended into heaven.
The vault was crumbling… the lightings were blazing,
And the birds did not understand his language.
When he is full of a passionate impulse,
Subject only to the sun and the moon,
He rushed amid the star tide
Where the secret remained deep.
In the chill of that cosmic font
He did not find the long-awaited goal!
In him lived the temptation of an unthinkable miracle,
But life evoked such dreams.

That he did not distinguish thin from good,
And in that I did not feel guilty.
So what are you, omnipotent nature?
You can't heal a crazy freak!
What he was what he seemed – everything was gone!
His mirage was woven of deception
He did not comprehend the desired moment,
When a guess burned him,

That the heart beat for nothing in these years,
In the confusion of feelings, in the tears of the past centuries!

Having sipped full of worries, needs, doubts,
He sank to the bottom with a shark,
To terminate the connection over time.
In the depths of those he was deaf and dumb,
When in anguish, passionate and sad
I breathed one sea blue…
An unclear call, where is the change of days and years,
Chased, but life did not open –
The last phenomenon appeared
Deaf and dumb fish to him.
And with every hour the forces changed,
And soon the thread of life was cut…
This is the passage of time when everything is done
Suppressed… Night, emptiness, oblivion.
And at dawn on the wet shore
The body of an unknown man was found
The waves hummed him pushing
My sad melody.

Oh yes, the bottom line: let it be without deception.

Friends, the end of my Dunstan.
Even if this is a dream, and it is not full…
My hero is not that, kept by a wave,
I rushed about in life to a speck of visible dust,
Alas, not seeing an achievable goal,
That's where his madness and trouble lies!

Gypsy dreams

I no longer believe in spring dreams.
They cheat like gypsies.
I don't want to seem sinful
Believing the swarthy schemers.

What will not be prophesied in a dream?
Do I have gypsy dreams, sorcerers?
Do rivals sharpen their teeth?
What do the fairies want to tell me?

I don't understand the speech of gypsies,
Verb, that something important.
I'm tired of the arrogant tyrants
Sometimes they are terribly scary.

Gypsy dreams know something
Can't explain just plainly.
We do not understand each other
At least howl loudly to me like a grey wolf.

I don't believe in dreams – magic dreams,
My tit is dear to me.
The crane is a bird of the skies,
At least at night I dream more.

Miller Caldwell dreams of pets and animals from time to time and here is another dream about Kofi, his intelligent West African Grey Parrot. Oh, how he misses him.

The Missing Parrot

It was after I stubbed my finger on a stubborn door bell, this dream took place. Earlier in the day, I had found myself in A&E being attended for a mallet finger. My middle finger now wore a splint. As a consequence, my erect middle finger was offensive if I held it up to the world. It was uncomfortable at times in bed but did not stop this dream.

I found myself returning home after my hospital visit that day with an extra splint given to me when I told the nurse about my amazing parrot. She told me these splints were indestructible and so it would be ideal and of interest to Kofi. But when I returned home, my dream was underway. I found the lounge door open and Kofi's cage open. I raced upstairs and checked all rooms. He was often in the bathroom watching me shave in the morning but he was not there. I called his name out, but there was no reply. I returned downstairs with an audible heart beat. Then I broke into a sweat in seeing the conservatory door ajar and I realised, with dread, that Kofi had joined his friends in the sky.

I ran about the garden and called his name while looking for any swaying branches. But it seemed he had taken an inquisitive flight far beyond the sanctuary of his cage, our garden, our town perhaps? I phoned the police to report a missing parrot. I was told a parrot had been seen in the grounds of the local hospital. It must have come to the hospital to look for me, of course. I drove out to the hospital there and then, speeding around 100 mph to get there quickly. The car's tyres squeaked and screeched as I took tight corners. I drove through red traffic lights. Fortunately, the traffic cops were nowhere to be seen.

I walked round the hospital grounds calling 'Kofi, Kofi' to the branches. There were many more trees by the mental health wards. I ventured near them and again called my pet's name. A young man came out of the hospital and approached me. 'You looking for coffee?'

'Yes,' I said with a smile as the light was fading. 'Kofi, where are you?'

'Come with me. I could do with a warm cup of coffee too,' the man said. I was having no luck finding my missing bird and I knew, as it was quite dark, Kofi would be roosting on a branch somewhere.

I accepted the man's invitation for coffee in the ward office as he sorted his papers. Then he telephoned a doctor. 'Can you section him? Well, he's been speaking to trees and asking them for coffee.'

I struggled to break free but two men in white coats arrived and took me into a ward where pyjamas were neatly laid at the end of a bed. I was instructed to get in them because it would be an early start I'd need, to find coffee in the branches the following day. I relaxed in bed feeling they were doing me a good turn after all. But when I woke the following morning it was a different shift and a large rotund nurse saw me dress. 'Where are you going, mate?' he growled at me. I told him I was ready to resume my search for Kofi in the trees.

'Oh no you're not. You're waiting for Dr Ffrench-Blake's morning round before you are going anywhere.'

'But I'm not a patient. I'm not mentally ill,' I protested.

'That's what they all say in here. Now get back into bed and await the doctor.' His command was so strong I could not refuse. I looked at my fellow bed companions. Many had no teeth, only gums.

'You'll get coffee later in the day,' shouted one and all heads nodded their agreement. I took that as a sign of support from the patients. Daylight came to me when curtains were pulled back. Dr Ffrench-Blake the psychiatrist was doing his ward round. Grateful patients swallowed the green liquid medication or the handful of pills on offer. Eventually the doctor arrived at my bed and looked through his notes. He looked confused. I told him I was looking for my lost parrot and by mistake I found myself in a mental hospital. 'I am really not ill', I told him.

'And neither you are,' he replied. 'I heard about your missing parrot on the 7 am news this morning. I hope you find your parrot soon. What was its name?'

'Kofi, it is,' I informed him.

He smiled at me and nodded his head.

'Too early for coffee,' shouted a bed mate. But the psychiatrist's diagnosis did the trick.

I left the mental hospital and returned home dejected. I opened the door and saw to my amazement Kofi climbing his metal pole to his open cage. I relaxed.

I awoke.

'**Hi Miller,**' writes a former colleague. No, I was never an estate agent either.

I rarely remember much of my dreams, but occasionally they come in a more cinematic and memorable format. And lo, during Friday night this is what I experienced:

A COUNTRY HOUSE

I was telling someone that most of the potential buyers for the country house I was selling were being put off by something. Then a whole flurry of letters arrived, from different people but in identical terms and all wanting to buy with each other. So we arranged a meeting in a big room in the house. The buyers sat at tables round three sides of a square - maybe 20 or 30 of them. I sat with other people, probably people who were helping with the sale, at a table in the middle. The buyers all wanted to buy and said Aunt Maud would pay. Aunt Maud, wearing 1960s or 70s tweeds, smiled and agreed.

Then they said: you can see what we're going to do to the house if you go behind the curtain and pull yourself up the rope. I noticed that the big curtains over the middle windows in the room were pulled shut. A couple of other people did it, and reappeared with big smiles. I tried, and found myself stuck looking out of a window on a dark sky with the faintest line of light on the horizon - but somehow I knew the light was not going to change and I was stuck there for good.

And then I woke up! I can't tell you any more than that. Did I own the country house, or was I merely the estate agent? No idea.

Kevin McCann is "One of the best poets in the country…" – so wrote Jimmy McGovern. "Kevin provides that extra wow factor." *Times Educational Supplement*. He has worked extensively with schools and youth groups throughout the whole of the country. He was writer - in - residence in H.M.P. Birmingham (for the Arts Council of England) and H.M.P. Wymott (for both the Poetry Society and the Gulbenkian Foundation), he appeared as a character in a novel and had a poem included in *The Lakes* by Jimmy McGovern. He has run poetry workshops and given readings in schools, prisons, community centres, libraries, hospitals, universities, cafes and pubs. EDUCATIONAL EXPERIENCE: English and Drama teacher for sixteen years + Lecturer in Creative Writing at Liverpool University, Dept. of Continuing Education for ten years.

The Haunted House

There was this haunted house. All the kids said it was anyway and there were all kinds of stories. The main one, I mean the one everyone said was like the real true story was that this mean old biddy had done in this kid and then buried him in the cellar. They said he haunted the place because no one had ever found his body and he wouldn't rest easy till they did. There were other stories as well. Like if you went by the place and its shadow touched you, you'd die in a year. So we used to cross over the road and pass on the other side. One time, my mate Chris swore he'd seen a face at one of the upstairs windows but nobody really believed him. He was well known for lying ever since he said he'd got a grip of Jane Walmsley. He'd have no chance with her and we all knew it.

Anyway, when I asked him to say what this face looked like, he got a bit vague and suddenly he was all *It was getting dark* and *I couldn't really see* until, in the end, I just came straight out and said, "Yer just makin' this up."

Well then he got really angry and said he'd put me on me arse if I ever called him a liar again. I told him he couldn't put my sister on her arse and he said he already had. I didn't get what he meant for a second but then everyone else started laughing and suddenly, I knew exactly what he meant. So I hit him as hard as I could in the stomach. As he doubled up, I gripped his ears and brought my knee up into his face with a crack. He went down and I was about to punch the air triumphantly when I felt my wrist grabbed and was dragged round to face an angry looking teacher.

I got six even though Chris told them it was a fair fight and he'd started it. He only got three because Mr. O'Fallon said going through life with a bent nose for evermore was probably punishment enough to be going on with.

Fortunately, most of Chris' blood had gone on his dark blue blazer so it blended in nicely. Course the cane hurt and as long as my hands were swollen red and stinging hot, I didn't feel very friendly towards anyone, let alone Chris so we left it there.

That afternoon, after school, I walked back home by the haunted house. As I got closer, I could see some Collegiate Girls standing on the pavement opposite. One of them was pointing. Now the house's shadow lay right across the pavement and I was about to swerve across the road so as not to walk through it when I saw the girls all looking at me. So I waved, kept walking right through the shadow and out the other side. I thought they might be impressed. I thought wrong. They glared at me and one of them shouted, "You're stupid you! You're just stupid!"

Now I knew Collegiate Girls weren't like us. They were Proddies for one thing. In fact, we'd even been warned to stay away from them by the Christian Brothers on account of them being immoral. But the way she reacted was crazy. I mean, we all went along with the haunted house routine the same way we went along with Mass and Baby Jesus. In other words, nobody really believed it.

In fact, Mark Harrison reckoned that the Christian Brothers couldn't really believe in it. "Cos if they did," he explained, "it'd mean there really is a Hell and they'd all be brickin' it right now over the things they've done." Out of the mouths of babes, as they say; anyway, back to the girls. The one who'd shouted pointed at me again. "You idiot!" she screamed then burst into tears. That worried me. Last girl I reduced to tears had had a very big brother. I decided valour was the better part of discretion, crossed over the road and began walking towards them.

That was the next surprise. I could see, as I got a bit closer, that they were all obviously about sixteen. I was only just turned fourteen so sixteen year old girls were your mates' older sisters, the ones you secretly fancied who always cut you dead. Either that or they were the ones who roamed town in packs on Saturday afternoon looking for insecure adolescent lads to ritually humiliate at bus stops. But sixteen year olds who believed in curses and all that…it had to be a wind up…had to be. Only, it wasn't. This girl was crying real tears, lots of them and loudly too. "Er, look," I began. "I'm really sorry I've upset you. It was just a joke." And I was. Now I was up close I could see she was fit and a blonde too.

One of her friends turned on me. "Oh go way, you stupid fool," she hissed, "can't you play your games somewhere else?" Then she took a step forward and spat on the ground at my feet. This was getting ugly and I wanted to give it legs but I didn't.

I stood my ground. "Why you spittin' at me? I haven't done anything."

"You wouldn't understand," the spitter said. "You're too young. Now get lost!"

So I did.

It wasn't until the following Friday that our paths crossed again. It was Autumn half-term. None of us could understand it. The CB's weren't known for their kindness so we were a bit surprised when Old Mother Riley (aka Brother Ignatius Riley) announced in morning assembly that we could all go home straight after lunch. Mark Harrison reckoned he was probably just pissed again – we'd all noticed that the smell of drink coming off him was getting earlier by the day – so we all cheered and Harrison shouted "We love ya Riley!" so's he wouldn't change his mind.

Me and Chris were off down the school drive and out the front gate within five minutes of the morning bell going. Chris was going straight home. He claimed he was meeting a bird later and needed to hang onto his readies. I decided to go into town for a mooch; me, mum and dad were both in work (most people were back then) so I was in no rush to get home.

I decided to swing by Smokey Joe's – so called because proprietor Joe was a chain smoker – and have a look through the latest LP's I couldn't afford. No CD's back then; but Smokey Joe's was shut for lunch so I decided to head for the Market instead. There was a stall there sold second hand books and batches of Yank comics dirt cheap. I was officially too old for comics – in other words me mum had decided I wasn't allowed to read them. No problem though. I just smuggled them into the house and hid them inside me Junior Encyclopaedias.

When I got to the Market, it was pretty busy. Friday lunchtimes always were but all the queues were at the greengrocers' stall, the fishmongers, the butchers…the bookstall was empty. There was a lot of pulp fiction paperbacks with the kind of graphic lurid covers guaranteed to give you some very sticky dreams. Right next to them were the comics; which was great because you could pretend to be browsing the comics whilst surreptitiously committing some raunchy looking woman's cleavage to memory.

And I was doing just that when, "You dirty little sod!" stung my ears and I turned round to see her, that girl, standing behind me, her face contorted with disgust. I felt myself go red.

"I don't know what you mean," I said trying my best to sound indignant and bewildered all at the same time.

She laughed, "Yes you do, standing there pretending to look at the Batman comics and all the time gettin' an eyeful."

"I wasn't!"

"Yes you were. You're not old enough to be looking at stuff like that." Here she paused and then said, "How old are you anyway?"

"Sixteen," I lied then added, "Nearly."

She laughed again, "What, fifteen and three quarters is it? Cos if that's true aren't you too old for comics?"

I noticed a couple of women queuing at the Fishmongers opposite were now looking across and the guy who ran the stall had put down his paper and was watching with barely concealed amusement. "I think she's gotya there, lad!" he said.

I clutched the last straw available. "Yes, well, what's it got to do with you anyway?" It was pathetic. I knew it. She knew it and by now the entire queue at the Fishmongers knew it. I was burning up with shame, embarrassment, anger and wanted out. I was also getting dangerously close to tears. I didn't trust myself to speak so just turned away and stalked out of the Market. I was followed by a lot of laughter.

My lips felt like they were twisting themselves into knots, my eyes stung and my throat had shrunk down to half its normal size. I was about to step straight into the road – in fact one foot was already on the road – when I felt a hand on my shoulder jerk me back fully onto the pavement, heard an angry shout from the driver of a car that swerved to avoid me and that girl's voice saying, "For Christ's sake…" What I wanted to do was tell her to just leave me alone but I still couldn't trust myself to speak so glared instead. She didn't glare back. Instead she said quietly, "Did nobody ever tell you to look before you cross the road?" I shrugged her hand off my shoulder and (still breathing heavily through my nose) said, "Leave me alone all right, just leave me alone!"

I went to cross the road again only this time I did look. There were cars solid in both directions so instead I set off walking past the big Post Office and in the general direction of Central Library - and she set off with me.

"Look," she began quietly, "I'm sorry I upset you. It was tight." Now that almost stopped me dead in my tracks. Older kids never said sorry for anything. I didn't know what to say. We were just by the pie shop so I said, "I'm going in here," in the hope she'd get the message and get lost. Didn't work though; she just followed me in. I bought a pork pie and my plan was to leg it while she was buying whatever she was buying. Only that didn't work either. She just stood there while I was being served and then walked straight out with me.

The thing is though; I was calming down so broke the silence with, "You bunking off too?"

She smiled (she had a nice smile) and said, "No, we got out early." There was another silence then, "What's your name?"

"Patrick. What's yours?"

"Marion"

I opened up the paper bag I was carrying and held it out towards her… "Do you wanna bite of me pork pie?" She began laughing. I felt myself getting angry again, "What's so funny?"

"Oh nothing," she said smiling again, "God, you're touchy aren't you?"

"I don't like people laughing at me."

"My brother didn't…" she began then stopped suddenly and when I looked at her, I could see she was getting all tearful which threw me into panic mode. I didn't know what to say so followed me dad's advice and said nowt. I put the bag in my pocket and we walked on in silence. I felt a spot of rain on my face followed rapidly by several more so broke the silence with, "Starting to rain." There was a cafe just over the road. "We could go in there for a cup of tea or something." I paused again and then added, "I've got money."

She pulled a paper hankie out of her sleeve – girls always seemed to have paper hankies up their sleeves – blew her nose and said, "So've I, so we'll go Dutch."

The café was pretty empty. We got a seat by the window and she ordered a pot of tea for two. Once that arrived and we'd let it stand for a minute or two to brew, she poured. I sat there silently hoping someone I knew would walk past and see me in the company of an actual girl who wasn't my sister when she broke the silence with, "Do you believe in curses?"

"What, you mean voodoo dolls and pins and all that? No it's bollocks."

She looked a bit taken aback, "But I thought all you Catholics believed in cured at Lourdes and rosary beads and holy pictures…"

"I'm not a Catholic anymore," I said proudly, "I'm an atheist."

"That why you walked through that shadow? You're not scared summat's going to happen to you?"

Chance to impress, I thought so said, "Curses only work if you believe in 'em."

"My brother thought that," she said, "and he even went in there to show he weren't scared."

"In the house you mean?"

"Course in the house…" she paused again and took a swig of tea. Her hands were shaking a bit and she spilled some on the table. I was about to go and get a serviette from the main counter to mop it up when she started talking.

"It were when I were in Juniors and he was in Grammar School. He used to collect me and bring me home cos me mum and dad were working. Any road, I told him some of the kids in school were saying there was this ghosty house and if its shadow touched you, you'd die.

"He told me that were rubbish and it was just an old dump that were falling down that tramps used for a toilet. He said he'd looked in it once and there were nothing there and to prove it, he took me past it on our way home from school one day, crossed over road and walked right through the shadow and said 'see look, nowt 'appens!' but then when he was coming back over to me, he din' look properly and this car almost 'its 'im and the driver's all 'watch where yer goin' and 'a could a killed yer!'

"He were a bit shook up but laughed it off only next day in school he were playing Five-a Side and went over and sprained his ankle."

"But that was just…" I began but she cut across me with, "Who's telling this story!" and she was so loud the bloke at the counter looked up from his paper so I zipped it.

"And then it went on," she continued, "one accident after another. Anyway, one night he comes back from his mate's house and he were dead quiet. Me dad noticed and kept saying 'what's up with you?' and he kept saying 'nothing' but me dad wouldn't let up so in the end he says that his mate had a Ouija Board. Me mum went spare at him but me dad calms her down and says to me brother, 'what do you want to go messin' with them things for?'

"Anyway the next thing, me brother's in tears so, me dad asks him what happened. Well then he tells us the Ouija Board says he gonna get murdered and he's dead scared cos now he thinks it's true. Me dad tells him it's all a load of crap and it was probably his mates just trying to scare him by pushing the thing around, you know, that spells out words.

"After that he wouldn't go out. He'd take me to school and pick me up again at the end of the day but apart from that he never set foot; stayed in the house all the time. He got thin as well. This went on for weeks and in the end me mum gets the Vicar to come round. That didn't do any good either.

"And then one day, he seemed back to his old self and all the way to school he were dead cheerful. When he dropped me off, he give me some money for sweets. I thought he'd gone on to school only it turns out he didn't. He bunked off and went back home. Me mum and dad had gone to work and he must have used his key to get back in the house. Me mum had these sleeping pills…" and she suddenly stopped and started crying, only quiet like so the bloke at the counter never noticed.

I knew what was coming but I said nowt and waited. I didn't have to wait long. She wiped her cheeks with the back of her hand and then went on. "Thing is, me mum were in work and she said afterwards she'd had this feeling so told the boss she weren't well and rushed back home…only it were too late. He was already…" and then she broke down again. This time the bloke at the counter did notice and he was straight down to us like a shot.

He wasn't angry. He spoke to her quiet like and asked what was up and if I'd upset her. She just shook her head and then managed to say, "I've had some bad news." As soon as she said that he went and got her another brew and said how sorry he was for her trouble. Then he left us in peace. She drank her tea in about three gulps and then I went up to pay but he wouldn't take me money and told me to get something nice for the girl.

When I got back to our table, she was already standing up and said, "I'd better get off home now. Me mum worries if I'm late back."

I was planning on walking her to the bus stop or back home but as soon as we got outside she said, "See ya," and started to walk off. I caught up with her and said, "Will I walk you home?" She stopped and shook her head. "No thanks, I just want to be on me own."

So I stood and watched as she vanished into the afternoon shoppers. After that, I'd sometimes see her in town. She'd nod and say hello and then one day she was holding hands with this lad and pretended she hadn't seen me. He did though and said something to her so she waved.

And then I never saw her again.

Kevin's next dream

Dear Miller,

As promised I dream a lot and remember a lot of them & even have vivid ones in which I know I'm dreaming but here's one I had years ago which has stayed with me.

I'm walking down an empty street and meet a large white horse – it stops in front of me and talks – it indicates a building in the street with a movement of its head – the building is old red brick and looks like a technical college and tells me to go and study. I ask the horse its name and he (I realise it's a he) replies "Rabbi" as I stare at his face it seems to shift and become human. It's a long thin face with large eyes and grey hair and I know I know him from somewhere…then I wake up.

A few days later I was in a second hand bookshop and came across a biog of Pasternak. Inside was a photo taken a few years before he died. It was the face from my dream.

Since then I've read everything I can by or about Pasternak - I've even written two poems about him – one of which is I think the best poem I've ever written. He remains a source of inspiration.

Regards,
Kevin

On the day after (i.m. Boris Pasternak)
On the day after he died
Pravda gave extensive coverage
To something else.

On the day after he died

A hand written sign giving funeral
Details is briefly displayed
At his local station: a beacon fire:
Which within an hour is answered
By others flaring right down the line
So now dozens defiantly file
Through his dacha,
Some kneel,
Many sob angrily
As they carry him shoulder high
Open casket flower brimming:
His final stroll across an open field.

Night Terror (after Pasternak)

Trees in their motley
Are reflected back
From wall mirror
Onto windowpane
Then reflected back again,
Overlapping images of the dead
He's yet to meet and the ones
He mustn't name: their light
Pours down walls, dust covers
Drip melting, floorboards crack
Into floes and his syllables
Flock like starlings: he wakes up:

It's Autumn, still raining,
First light's cold and thin:
Another night lived through:
No one way ride at three a.m.

And then One Morning:

He comes downstairs
To find
All the kitchen chairs
Re-arranged
In a semi-circle
Facing
The locked back door,
Coats and jackets
Off their hooks
Piled up on the floor,
Hears from upstairs
Creaking floorboards,
Tuneless singing,
Switches on the radio,
Flicks on the kettle
As Ray Davies asks
"What are we living for?

Very lyrical

He clears his throat and begins to read:
"I'd walk the tide-line pocketing shells,
Carefully side-step beached jellyfish,
Race my own shadow as far as the pier,
Get up to the prom for a massive ice-cream:
It was a Summer dream…"
Carefully she waits until silence

Has stretched just long enough
And tongue unknotted chimes in with:
"One year we stayed in an old caravan
Only our money's got lost
But Mum finds ten bob so Dad has a bet,
Well, long story short his long-shot romps
Home at a hundred to one so for the rest
Of that week we picnicked
On the sandy beach,
Played Pontoon for pennies
And Jesus how we laughed…"
"But that's not my memory!"
He vainly protests.
"Oh it will be by your next poem," she says.

Kevin Patrick McCann

Andrew Goss is an international humanitarian and journalist. He is the author of the novel *The Humanitarian* and lives in Leicester. His dream is that one day the poorest across the southern hemisphere is freed from poverty through greater quality of opportunity and fairer distribution of wealth – and that we finally live as one. He hopes to return to Pakistan one day. But first Eritrea.

A Touch of Fever

HE AWOKE WITH a pounding head and stared up through narrowed, bleary eyes at the white mosquito net stretched out like a veil above him in the early morning light. He'd had a troubled, restless sleep. His body too was aching.

For a few moments he lay there, taking in his surroundings, conscious of his own heartbeat and his breathing in the silence of the new day. He had woken before his alarm clock had sounded. And it was light. He therefore figured it must be sometime before 6.00am and 7.00am.

He decided to make an effort to climb from his bed and rolled over to unpeg the net with clumsy fingers. His senses were blurred, his head searing with pain, his limbs heavy and fatigued as he swung his legs out. He sat on the edge of the bed, hunched forward, his breathing laboured, slightly disorientated and uncertain of his next action.

Often he awoke with a heavy head and had become accustomed to taking regular painkillers to stave off blinding headaches. But this was different. He felt cold. And yet he realised he was sweating. "Bugger!" he muttered. He felt weak and tired. And he began to feel nauseous. He was still sitting on his bed when the alarm clock began to bleep and he stretched out an arm to silence it. The effort seemed too much and he slumped backwards onto the mattress. He lay there, staring up at the net and began to shiver. He was thirsty too, but now seemed unable to raise himself. He closed his eyes as his grip on reality diminished and he sank into a feverish state of light and shadow.

Cousins was still lying there when he became vaguely aware of the knocking on his door. Yet he seemed unable to respond from the dreamlike state somewhere between sleep and consciousness in which he now found himself. He heard African voices. He felt the touch of cool fingers upon his forehead. More voices. This time female. And then it seemed he was falling, dropping into a deep, dark and bottomless chasm…

***

Hannah Johnson was bent over Cousins as he lay in his bed. She sat on the edge of the mattress watching him, listening to the laboured sound of his breathing. His eyes were closed, but seemed to flicker as if perhaps he was dreaming. It was a handsome face, she mused, as she studied its features, though clearly the man was ill. There were dark rings beneath his eyes. The cheeks were gaunt and already there was the shadow of several days' beard growth.

His skin was pallid and there were small beads of sweat upon his forehead.

He had slept for large periods of time during the day. Sometimes he had spoken in his sleep; anxious, meandering mutterings of fear, or deep sadness as the fever and the shivers persisted. But there had been periods of lucidity too, when he had been able to raise his body to sit up in bed to drink. Slowly and with assistance. But then he would feel the need to rest again and he would sink back into a restless, troubled sleep. The fever had not yet broken.

Johnson had been a regular visitor. She sighed before reaching forward and dabbing his forehead with the cool cloth in her hand. Then she looked up at the figure standing beside her. Walters watched her pensively, with knitted brow, a look of concern upon his face.

"He seems better," she said.

The doctor took a deep breath. "But we can't leave it much longer," he said. "Another day, perhaps… if the fever and delirium continue, we're going to have to get him to hospital. We can't take the risk. And most likely they'll want to play safe," he added.

"I know," she replied absently and wiped Cousins' forehead again. She knew Walters was right. Perhaps they had been wrong to delay. Malaria was one of the biggest killers in Eritrea. Though the illness was less severe in adults, it killed children in their thousands. It remained a dangerous hazard for the Westerners who came to work, not just in Eritrea, but across sub-Saharan Africa. They had no immunity to the parasite. And it hit those who developed symptoms hard. Often they would need to be hospitalised. Some were repatriated; the severest cases could cause complications that were fatal. But they were rare.

There was no real protection. The side effects of anti-malarial medication were too harsh for many. Prolonged usage could damage the nervous and immune systems. The skin would break down, or the eyes would become oversensitive to light. Sometimes the effects were permanent. So you took your chance. The best protection was a mosquito net, repellents and scanning your room day and night for any sign of the insects. And, of course, keeping your skin covered. But it was something of a gamble.

The blood tests indicated Cousins had contracted what was termed 'uncomplicated malaria'. It was not the severest form of the disease. That was a relief. And emergency treatment had started immediately with Artemisinin tablets. The fever should break within the next day, or so. And he might then slowly regain his strength over the next few days, if he rested. That was the hope. But there was always a small element of doubt.

So far his raging temperature had fluctuated. And the delirium too had been intermittent. There was no coma. And that was good. The patient had even seemed cheerful at times, sitting up in bed when his fever subsided a little.

And he was adamant he did not want to leave Eritrea. Yet in reality, it was out of his hands. That would be for the head of mission to decide. If he was no better within the next twenty-four hours, the decision would be made for him. He'd be admitted to the nearby hospital. And there was still a vague possibility of complications. No one would want to take that chance.

But for now he was being attended by Walters and Johnson at the request of the British NGO he was working for. The international medics shared their compound in Asmara with the British and their staff had agreed to keep a close eye on the 'patient'. And the Englishman dutifully took the large blue and white capsules offered with water that would cleanse his blood of the parasites which had infected his blood.

"I'll sit with him for a while," Johnson said.

Walters nodded. "I'll see you later," he replied and turned to leave the room. He paused at the door. "But if he is no better in the morning, we'll have to take him to the hospital."

"Yes David," she replied absently, watching Cousins, whose eyes were still closed. He seemed unaware of her presence. She rose from his bed, pulled the net across and then drew up a wicker chair. Outside the sun was beginning to set. She'd stay with him until darkness fell.

***

Cousins was far away. In his dreamlike state he was back in Pakistan, re-living the loss that had led him to Eritrea. It was his worst nightmare, though he rarely dreamed about it now, even though it still haunted him.

He'd loved her. Afsa Ali had been his life. And he hadn't seen the signs. He was working away in the Punjab when the message came to him. She needed him. And yet in his dream he was unable to reach her. When finally he arrived home she had seemed different. Distant.

"I need you here," Ali had told him. She too was working, spending long hours away in the 'field', often writing her reports until the early hours. It was taking its toll. He decided to step back from the work which took him away from the family home to help care for their little boy. Yet she could give up her own work, he suggested, if it was too demanding. They didn't need the money.

She had insisted she continue. He knew only it was work that took her away from him, somewhere in the northwest alongside the UN. She would return home to Islamabad at the weekends exhausted. Even then she continued to work. It was like a spiralling obsession. It was an opportunity she could not give up, even though it was pushing her to the brink of a 'burnout'. He'd seen it before in others. And he was worried.

She became cold, emotionally distant; secretive, even. It was as though she was becoming a different person, almost unrecognisable. The intimacy they had known together was gone. At times, she even seemed to despise him. Yet he felt powerless. The more he tried to help her, the more she seemed to push him away. In her head he had become the enemy. Then one day she told him.

"I don't think I love you anymore; you add nothing to my life." It was a statement that lacked any emotion, or compassion. Then she smiled. He was stunned and hurt. What did she mean? They had argued. But she maintained her distance. She told him he had failed her. He didn't understand. Her work seemed the only thing of value to her. Not even their little boy seemed important. And he, least of all. The woman he loved so deeply was disappearing before his very eyes, tottering on the brink of breakdown.

They were still sleeping together, though the physical and emotional intimacy had gone. Sometimes, though, when she lay sleeping, he would watch her in the early morning light. It was only in those moments that her face relaxed and some of its softness would return. And in her sleep she might lean towards him, or even reach out to him. But it would sadden him, for even in his dream he knew the closeness would pass. The hardness would return in the cold light of day. It was a look which broke his heart. And once more the distance would be there, which was a gap he was unable to bridge.

Then one night he found himself sleeping alone. In the darkness he could see a rectangle of burning light which framed the adjoining bathroom door. And for a while he lay there, unable to move, his heart filled with a sense of dread. When she did not return he was finally able to force himself to rise from his bed and approach the light framing the bathroom door. Yet as he stood there he could hear nothing. He knocked, but there was no response. He knocked again, a little louder. Nothing. Now worried, he forced the door, pushing all his weight against it until it gave way. And suddenly he was presented with the terrible scene he had feared most of all.

She lay in the bath, slumped within the blood-red water in which her naked body lay, her head to one side, her life ebbing slowly from the deep cuts to her wrists.

"Oh my God," he heard himself utter in despair as he found himself watching the scene play out like a detached, out-of-body observer. He saw himself rush forward. His one overpowering thought: "God, please let me not be too late." He watched himself stoop over the bath and lift her from the water into his arms. The wounds were deep. He watched his desperate self clutch frantically for towels and press them over the lacerations, cradling her to him. He saw her slowly open her eyes.

"I'm sorry," she murmured. The coldness was gone and there was an overwhelming rush of love for the woman in his arms.

"It's all right, baby," he heard himself say with mounting despair. "Hold on. Please. Hold on!"

"So very sorry," she repeated, gazing into his eyes as he held her.

"It's OK," he told her. "It's going to be OK." And she smiled faintly. But he now knew the life was slipping from her.

"Sorry I couldn't love you better…" she said, almost in a whisper.

His mind was racing, his heart pounding. And he felt the tears begin to blur his eyes.

"I know you loved me as well as you were able," he heard himself say, his voice trembling with emotion. And she closed her eyes for the last time.

"It's all right… my darling it will be all right…" he told her. But the life had gone from her and her body lay limp in his arms. And then he began to sob and shake uncontrollably. His heart was breaking.

***

He cried out loud as he awoke. And as he lay under the net blinking in the soft light he realised he was crying. Hannah Johnson awoke too with a start, still sitting in the wicker chair where she had fallen asleep. In the light of the lamp she could see Cousins, although his eyes still seemed to be closed. She pulled back the net to see his face was wet with tears. And then he opened his eyes and gazed up at her.

"Are you all right?" she asked him.

"Bad dream," he answered. "Painful memories."

"I'm sorry," she said, reaching across to put her hand gently upon his forehead, which was cool to her touch. The fever had broken.

"Welcome back, John," she smiled. And he too was smiling.

99 Lashings

Miller Caldwell

This dream came to me while awaiting the final entry for this book. I have worked in Pakistan and been to Oman but this dream came to me from Iran, where I have never set foot.

I was arrested in the hotel room by the Iranian police on a charge of rape. I denied any knowledge of this offence. Nevertheless I appeared in court the next day to deny the offence.

At court I was given no legal representative so I chose to defend myself. The alleged victim was first to give her account. I deceived her immediately.

'I am the defence lawyer. Have we ever met?'

'No, sir.'

'I am European. Do you not recognise me?'

'No, sir, we have never met.'

'Exhibit A on the table is written in your hand is it not?'

She looked at her statement. 'Yes I wrote it.'

'It is an account of your rape is it not?'

'Yes it is.'

'Where was this statement taken?

'At my house.'

'Did you request the police to visit you at your home?

'They always do.'

'I don't understand what you are saying?'

'This is the third time they have come to my home. I have given three statements, so far.'

'Are they all rape allegations?'

'Yes.'

'May I ask how often have you been raped?'

'I've never been raped.'

'Are any of the police officers who interviewed you in court today?'

'Yes, Mr Malik.'

'Can you point to him?'

She does so.

'Thank you. You may sit down. I call upon Mr Malik.'

'Mr Malik you attended the home of the victim. Who sent you to her home?'

'I don't know.'

'It's not a hard question. Presumably you were at your police station or in your police car and you were instructed to return to this lady's home. Who gave the order?'

Mr Malik took his time to answer but it was well worth the wait. 'The order came from the secret police.'

'And have the secret police asked you before to obtain a statement from the victim?'

'Yes three times.'

'And was each occasion a rape allegation?'

Mr Malik was crunching his cap as he struggled with an answer.

'I remind you that you swore an oath to Allah, Peace be upon Him, was each occasion a rape allegation?'

'Yes each was a rape.'

'Thank you, Mr Malik. You may stand down.'

'And, my dear Judges, that is the case. Indeed there is no case. There is no evidence linking me to any rape. I further contend there was no rape of anyone.'

I sat down as the three judges met in a huddle.

'We have come to our conclusion. By a majority, we find you guilty of rape. On Friday after prayers, you will be taken to Baharestan Square in Tehran where you will receive 99 lashings by a whip.'

'So the Judiciary are under the special police too. There is no evidence in this case.'

'Take him away.'

I counted the days down. They came very fast. On the dreaded Friday a car came to the police station and I was bundled into it. It took me back to my hotel room where I was asked to change back into my usual clothing and I had to have my passport returned from the front desk. I took out my wallet to pay for my stay but they said they were in a hurry and not to pay. I said if I don't pay the police will find another charge against me so they let me pay. The car took me to the Tehran airport. I asked what was happening. Apparently I was never going to be given 99 lashings. I was made an example of being one too many white business men in the country and some of them must have been spies, according to the secret police. They wanted to frighten me, which was all this dream was about. We shook hands and I boarded a flight to London, promising never to tell anyone what had happened. My lips are tightly sealed.

Merryn Glover writes fiction, drama, poetry and journalism. In a life spent crossing cultures, she was born in Kathmandu and brought up in Nepal, India and Pakistan. She went to University in Australia, keeps returning to South Asia and has called Scotland home for over 25 years. Her plays and short stories have been broadcast on Radio 4 and Radio Scotland and widely anthologised. Her first novel, *A House Called Askival* is set in an Indian hill-station and her second, *Of Stone and Sky*, in the upper Spey valley where she lives. Her current project is *The Hidden Fires: A Cairngorms Journey with Nan Shepherd*, Polygon 2022.

A Dream from Of Stone and Sky

When I finally fall asleep that night in the Green Bothy, I dream.

Everything is beautiful. I am walking around a vast stately home and there are elegant people drifting in and out of rooms and silent, bowing staff, and opulence. Rich carpets, chandeliers, mahogany, crystal, marble and gold. Perfect bodies are draped in silks and fine suits, jewellery glinting at ear and wrist, hair shining. As I walk I realise it is all mine and that everyone in some way belongs to me, friends, family, employees. They are a mix of people I know and people I've never seen before, and some of the strangers are my lovers and children, while some of the mute servants are my family. Moving up the grand staircase, I see the people change. Appetites rise, masks fall. A woman grabs a fistful of canapés and shoves them in her mouth, a man seizes a maid by the breast, a couple grope at each other in lust and spite. Up a flight and champagne flutes smash, dark stains spread on white shirts, make-up smears and teeth fall out. Higher and higher in the house the rooms become smaller and filthier and hotter, the people more grotesque, their decadence unfettered and cruel. Sometimes I look on in horror, sometimes

I am one of them, writhing like a maggot. I push on up, till I can barely move for old furniture stuffed everywhere, rotting mattresses and leering, disfigured faces. The heat is unbearable. Up a narrow wooden staircase in a tower, I find I am crawling through bodies that are amputated and bandaged, crushing and smothering me in their foul odours, their voices like distant, dying birds. Sweat pours off me, my clothes melt away, I reach for the door at the top and hear banging on it and shouting. As it crashes open, flames roar over me and the devil takes my throat.

An extract from the novel **Of Stone and Sky** *by Merryn Glover, Polygon Books, 2021. Used with permission.*

The late Paul Vuillermoz.

Brother of contributor Mathilde Vuillermoz, my friend and film agent. Paul Vuillermoz was ice climbing with two friends in the Secteur du Trient on the French Swiss border when an avalanche from high above ripped the three boys from the ice. Paul's two injured friends were able to dig themselves out but when they located the climbing rope, Paul was no longer attached. Rescuers found his body three days later.

It is no wonder that Mathilde often dreams about her brother whose love for iced climbing matched the love he had for his sister.

Dutch poet **Hannie Rouweler**. (Born in the Netherlands, at Goor, 13 June 1951), poet and translator, has been living in Leusden, The Netherlands, since the end of 2012.

Her sources of inspiration are nature, love, loss, childhood memories and travel. In 1988 she debuted with *Raindrops on the water*. Since then about 40 poetry volumes have been published, including translations in foreign languages (Polish, Romanian, Spanish, French, Norwegian, English).

Her poems have been translated in about 30 languages. She attended five years evening classes in painting and art history, at the art academy (Belgium). Hannie writes about a variety of diverse topics. 'Poetry is on the street, for the taking', is an adage for her. She mixes observations from reality with imagination and gives a point to her feelings and findings. Unrestrained imagination plays a major part in her works.

She has published a few stories (short thrillers); and is the editor of various poetry collections.

A comment

The poem, often emerging from reality, turns out to have wings, grabs for something higher, almost inimitable and almost untouchable and loses sight of reality. Then, via detours, via out-of-the-daily proportions, it returns to the ground, a plane that disappears into the clouds after take-off, an unearthly environment, after long periods of time descending on a runway. It is therefore very important to capture the flight path in words, especially if the landing is a remote island and rotating movements above water are necessary.

Hannie Rouweler

Dreams for Miller's dream book, in SCOTLAND.

Usually I dream in the morning, if I wake up early or else, I have forgotten it. If it is a nice dream, then I crawl back under the covers in the hope that the dream continues and develops, but that does not happen. Therefore, below a dream that I can still remember well, because it belongs to the chapter, recurring dreams. But this one was not nice.

I run down a long narrow corridor with doors in the side walls, which I want to open one by one. They are locked. I am being chased by something but cannot see clearly whether it is a wild bear or a man. I keep looking around and it gets closer. I keep running, pulling on doors and the moment the threat gets very close, the very last door flies open.

The Night is Sweet

Evening falls slowly on the lawn
where cats and people have disappeared into
their homes - I think of the quick sunset
in other parts of the world and the beach

where I am with you. You came back
to me. Where you come from doesn't matter.
Nothing matters anymore of a reason or memory
just this moment
that you are sitting next to me.
We watch the swell
from the waves, it is almost dark. Your shoulder
leans against mine and we merge
in this dreamtime, which was still given to us.

Marion de Vos-Hoekstra was born in the Netherlands and is married to a career diplomat. They both served in North Yemen, Tanzania, United Kingdom, Mali, Spain, South Africa and The United States and now have returned to the Netherlands. She trained as a teacher of French and as translator French, English and Dutch. She is also fluent in Spanish and German, plays the piano and the guitar, is an amateur ornithologist and makes drawings; aquarelles and oil paintings. Nature, human nature and her nomad life are her main inspiration. She attended several poetry workshops in English among which: a Master class in New York at Poetshouse and a course at the prestigious 92Y Institute. She is the author of five poetry collections (in English and Dutch), four with Demer Press, and is published in several anthologies and magazines (25) all over the world. (South Africa, Australia, UK and US.)

Her two poems are:
My Dream and Waking Up.

My Dream

I dreamed I was running with horses
hooves hovering above the earth,
I knew inevitably
my dream would be swallowed by daylight.

I dreamed I was strumming strings
without strain like a Flamenco guitar player,
I knew when night would turn into light
my dream had played a trick on me.

I dreamed I was painting
hallucinating colours, unseen before
I knew between wake and sleep,
my dream would evaporate by sunrise.

I dreamed I was singing the song of whales
like the whale caller
I knew when the veil of darkness lifted
my dream was one more illusion.
 I dreamed I was flying with migrating birds
from Arctic to Antarctic
I knew in my arising consciousness
my dream had failed me.

I dreamed I was writing
words, flowing and light
I knew, when morning dawned
my dream became my inspiration.

Waking up

Ready to bite:
those poisonous fangs
of a sand-coloured snake.

The crystal clear song
of a blackbird breaks
the ice of a January night,

reducing my snake
to savoury prey for
my black-coated saviour.

For a moment I believe
this song is for me
or for fate. No,

its sole purpose is:
to lure into its territory
a mate.

The Vegetable Prize

Miller Caldwell

This dream occurred in mid-winter 2021. The ground was as hard as iron, water like a stone. Yet my dream was a summer one, the warmth coming from the covers I clutched deep in sleep.

I was in an allotment. I'm not sure where but a row of terraced houses framed the growing area. I was not alone but other gardeners never raised their heads and no verbal interaction took place.

Amid the growing tomatoes, the rich green spinach, rows of regimented onions and the wayward wafting of green beans on their cane supports, was my pride and joy. It lay on a light bed of straw and its skin was as smooth as a baby's bottom. It shone in its cradle as I took out a measuring tape. Three feet, four inches in length it measured, with a girth of 23 inches. To me it was a perfect specimen of a fully grown vegetable marrow, an outgrown courgette.

It must have been Thursday because early on the Saturday morning, two days later, I returned to the allotment with a sharp knife. I knelt down and cut it neatly at its neck. I lifted it and placed it carefully in the linen bag I had brought for the occasion.

I took it home and washed it till all the small particles of detritus on its cover fell off and I polished it like a cricket bowler's ball. Three hours later I was at the Community Hall where tables were laid out and a chalk board listed the prizes and the donators. Most seemed to have died and left amounts of money to ensure a good selection of fruit and vegetables were on show each summer.

I was asked to display my marrow on a table marked 'Biggest on show'. That seemed appropriate. Before the judging got seriously underway, and serious were the well-tanned gardening experts, a man entered the hall with what seemed like a hockey bag. It was long and when it was unzipped, he brought out an ill looking marrow. I was relieved the yellow/brown pocked specimen did not match my bottle-green marrow. But his vegetable was put alongside mine. I screwed up my eyes. The lengths were about the same but the quality of mine would shine through. I was convinced.

Forty minutes later the judges, all three of them, arrived at our table. My excitement grew. The prize was £25 and that would go a long way towards an evening meal with my wife that evening. An inch tape was produced and the lengths recorded. The girths were measured too. And re-checked, quite unnecessarily, I felt. I easily won that element, surely? The judges nodded to one another. Then the chief judge gave her result. The winner for the longest length marrow, by a winning margin of only one quarter of an inch, goes to Mr Alan Nicolson. I froze. How could this have happened? Surely a quarter of in inch did not matter when the specimens could not have been more different.

Mr Nicolson stepped forward and received his £25 and I applauded politely, without much enthusiasm at his good fortune, and to show I was the contrite beaten finalist.

I lingered on to see other prizes being won. The best bunch of Tom Thumb tomatoes took the Margaret Bell trophy. The strangest looking carrot, gained the Thomas Sidebotham prize; the most luscious leaves of a lettuce, The Daisy Althrop cup and the length and freshness of stringer beans, the Connor McGrory prize. Each winner proudly came forward to collect their winning envelope. The event was coming to an end and a few had already left the hall.

Then the chief Judge made an announcement. 'And finally we come to the Best in Show. We have had an eye on all that have appeared this afternoon, both fruit and vegetables. Many have been a delight to see and much appreciation goes to the busy gardeners who have braved the elements to tend their crops. I can now announce that the winner of the Miss Massie Martin Prize for Best on Show and with the title of goes a cheque for £100…goes to…'

I felt TV was responsible for this elongated pause before any winner was announced. It seemed so inappropriate for a fruit and vegetable contest. Quite unnecessary. 'Goes to Mr Caldwell for his gigantic marrow.'

A broad smile widened my face and I stepped forward. I shook the Judges' hands and received not only my envelope but the Best on Show Cup. It reminded me of the FA winner's cup, so I held it aloft.

'And will you be cooking the marrow tonight, may I ask?' asked the judge.

'It's too big a marrow for the two of us,' I replied.

It was then I recognised a lady in the hall. She was clearly on her day off. Nevertheless, I felt she should have it.

'As I said, it would be too large a meal for us but perhaps the Apple Blossom Care Home should have it. Perhaps Mrs Pearson, if I give it to you, as Matron, you can take it to the chef at the Care Home and see what he can cook with it.'

Mrs Pearson came forward with a confident grin and received the vegetable with grateful thanks. I gave her the bag in which I had brought it, as I saw her struggle to hold it.

On the way home, I opened the envelope and saw the cheque for £100. I took my mobile phone and called my wife.

'Darling, don't cook anything tonight. We are going to celebrate.'

'What! Longest marrow?' she said, clearly pleased with my success.

'Longest. No I'm afraid I didn't win that competition.'

'Really?'

'Yes, Best in Show. That's why I can take you out this evening.'

That evening at Bruno's I asked for the stuffed marrow. It arrived looking like a courgette on the cusp of adolescence. But with its cargo of minced meat and mashed sweet potato, it certainly tasted good. I like my marrows.

I woke with a smile on my face. My wife asked me had I been dreaming again. I nodded.

'We are eating out tonight,' I said.

'What in lock-down?' she replied with a puzzled looking face.

'Oh well, let me go shopping. I'll make tonight's dinner. Do you fancy a marrow for tea?'

'Just a marrow?' she enquired.

Hannie Rouweler writes: I do not want to deny you one reaction. It comes all the way from Russia, Siberia in fact, from Eldar (poet, writer, mining engineer, polar explorer and researcher.) He informs me:

I have all the gifts for Christmas at home for my grandchildren, kept in a cupboard. Every year I let them know that they should give me a list of what they want. I forward that to Santa Claus in Lapland, and he comes early in the morning on his reindeer sleigh. A sleigh with wheels underneath, because if there is no snow, he cannot travel.

But now that they are have grown a bit older, they ask: I want to see him!! Can't he wait for me?

No, because he's way too busy.

Happy holidays, Hannie.

What follows is not a dream. It is an account of surviving Covid 19 in Serbia. I deem it appropriate as this book is being compiled in a Covid 19 Lock-Down and the narrative reminds us of the worldwide suffering that Covid 19 and its horrible successors have brought to every land.

Eldar is just out of hospital (Covid 19) in Russia's Siberia and
Hannie writes: I wish him a good recovery. It must have
been a shock to get through such a disastrous time. Eldar,
keep the faith, I admire your strength and for all: stay away
from hospitals if possible. In some European countries
doctors have to decide who they will help, and who not.

Stay safe, your friend, Hannie.

A SIBERIAN WARD –
ELDAR'S ACCOUNT

It looks different in the face of death. After surgery, I was placed
in a room for six people. I talked to them, they talked to me,
someone joked, and someone was silent: everything is as usual
between people. But with one huge difference: suddenly one
of the six was dying. So three people died. Two others were
seriously infected. At night, after 12 hours, orderlies came
for them and took them with them, as if they were taken to
execution   forever. After seven days, there were six people
in the ward again, but five of them appeared after me. Only
I remembered those who had been with me before.

The award winning poetry of **Rahim Karim Karimov** (Kyrgyzstan)

The poems of **Rahim Karim Karimov** can charm me, writes Hannie. That he is an important writer and poet can be deduced from bibliographical and biographical data, the many awards and the many nominations as poet of the year. You don't become that, easily. Scholars, connoisseurs and committees bend over much poetic work to give someone such an accolade.

That resonates throughout his oeuvre. It is also a sensitive voice, because, despite the fact that he firmly believes in God, in Allah, which recurs in his poems, there is also a desperate voice: that of the lonely and crying man in the desert. The despair of so much suffering and injustice in the world is there, to which he himself too, doesn't seem to escape. The shortcomings of love, the loss of a beloved one, the fears and loneliness.

In terms of content, each poem is convincing.

Rahim Karim Karimov's selection of Kyrgyzstan magical poetry follows.

Native poems

My poems are my relatives,
There is no one nearer anyone in the world to me.
How do I believe all your secrets?
And I can talk to you heart to heart.
I grew up with you, matured together,
Mine you are faithful reliable friends.
You are crying with me, and rejoice, sorry,
You were not happy: I was sad.
I do not know how life wasted without you,
I am not separated from you,
God sent me to you.
You – day and night with me: slept in verse,
Poems woke up: He became a man!
You replaced your mother, you were a sister,
You replaced father, brother to me.
You are my angels, sent by fate,
The candles were always in the dark for me.
Hope, support, strength
Saving my spirit like a magic amulet.
I will call you relatives today,
Dear, close, I will say thank you!
Do not leave my winged spirit
Please live with me until the last days.
Without you it's as if I have no legs, no arms,
Beating heart, you, my breath.

Lilac Volcano

In the gardens of the Earth there is a lilac salute,
Exploded as if a lilac volcano.
Caresses a honeyed sweet cosiness,
Will people scent people with such a fountain?
God gives us a lilac bouquet in the morning,
From the smell of flowers dizzy.
They sound like an echo – the white light is happy,
Earths are natural words of nature!
Do you fall in love with a lilac, oh, a drunken bee,
Kisses on the lips, without memory, mind.
The bee is intoxicated with a lilac scent,
Humanise the head of honey's fate?
As if the native land bloomed,
In the bushes lilac like a vine!
Beautiful as she, fragrant, good
I dare not take my loving eyes.

Syria and football.

And somewhere the children die, cry,
Blow up, cut, peaceful kill.
Pass somewhere indifferent matches,
Because of the ball, the peoples of the world are crying!
Oh, somewhere there are people without feet,
The whole world kicked the ball somewhere.
Because of the ball, everyone is crying, yes, everywhere,
No one for children, alas, does not cry!
Which went the world stale and insane,
All the people play carelessly in football.
For Syria does not want to cry,
For the ball want to cry all, soulless!
And somewhere a ball, where – the heads fly,
Men, women in the stadium…
The fans sit unceremoniously,
And somewhere the heads of people are kicking.
They are people – our brothers are with you,
And we're losing our heads!
Dazzling in their hands, flags on their faces – a banner. Are we
humans – robots, guys?

I am the ambassador!

In all, about, countries of the world
I am a poet, ambassador,
Over-pleinpotent, and, utterly extraordinary.
I have my own bread, my salt in the world –
People everywhere greeted my poems!
Ambassador I, not a single country,
I stand between nations, the races of the universe.
The Lord Himself appropriated to me this glorious rank,
Ambassador of Friendship I,
Peace in the countries of the whole Planet!

The Hedgehog

The hedgehog knows what life is in this world,
How terrible to live on it, in a circle of your kind.
Especially now, when it's slippery in the summer,
When around the bayonets, and stinging nettles.
When you need armour and insurance,
Repulse and defence must be prepared.
Friends, relatives as much as fake cheap things,
You must be on a check, on guard, at the ready!
Betrayal, treason all are capable now,
The hedgehog knows about this, because he is a philosopher!
Hedgehog, take care of yourself from treason, swine fever,
I envy you, my friend, my hedgehog is snub-nosed!
Oh, I would have your thorns – shields prickly, sharp,
From envious people and traitors, acquaintances.
As I understand you, my coat is colourful,
You are a symbol of caution, the creation of God!

Island of Purity.

I'm looking for an island of purity on the ground,
Seeking for light in the boat a land of kindness.
Around the water, raging waves, the ocean,
I search for years in the sea dryness of heat.
Well, where are you, show yourself, cherished, oh, stranded.
I'd like to see my own door as soon as possible.
One day I will discover an island of purity,
How Beruni opened a gap in America, a gap.

Without a friend the house is a dungeon.

As friendship is now in vogue,
And who is not friends – in sorrow.
The world is in every home,
Where friendship, happiness the sea.
Without a friend, the house is a dungeon,
And with a friend, heaven is a kibitka.
The poet wrote. Firebird,
She moves into the heart.
Without friendship – fear, anxiety,
In the hearts of people is hidden.
Without friendship it is very difficult,
Only friendship is kept honour.
Without friendship, grief, malice
Searing all souls. Without friendship,
It's stuffy in the wide world.
Without a friend, the house is a dungeon,
The master is poor, a beggar.
After all, friendship is a Firebird,
What is sent by the Almighty!

Autumn

Trees are silk dressing up,
Girls that were only yesterday.
Green, like schoolgirls in the yard,
We went to school in uniform all in the morning.
Today they suddenly dressed in chiffon,
Of the leaves of their multi-coloured outfit.
Orange and yellow, red background,
Are they rushing to the Pervomaysky parade?
And on the face a colourful make-up,
In the blush cheeks, lips scarlet ......
In a moment, the landscape changed,
But they will become naked in the future...
Brides in fact it will be time to come –
Undress the trees in November.
Throw silly good silk,
To put on that wedding in December.

Medical lie

How do we deceive ourselves?
For what is not averse to falling into hell.
We often lie to all of us,
As Hippocrates himself lied to the sick then.
Whom doctors take the oath to all:
"I will direct the patient to benefit,
I will not cause harm to health,
Who is ill hopeless on this day.
We swear by Apollo, not to kill,
We swear to keep silent about the secrets we have. We Swear
Mankind Love,"
But we will not lie forever, alas.
We lied to my mum, life to save her,
We lied to my dad, not to hurt him…
Now we have a time to take,
Trouble from relatives and relatives,
Lord! I do not know how many we'll still lie,
Doctor Asclepius at your own risk, fear?
To help people in the world to die,
Forgive us for your sins, forgive me, Allah!
Forgive the doctors, and with us,
When lies are better than the truth at this hour.
When the good of lies is useful phrases,
Truthful, faithful – purer than any rhinestones.
Medical lie, holy like a lie.

A Spaceship Incident

Miller Caldwell

I recall being in a spaceship. How I got there or why I was in the craft, I really can't explain. There was a crew of four and me. There were two Russians, one Chinese astronaut and an American and me. We all spoke English, enough to be understood, with heavy national accents.

We were returning from a visit to Jupiter. We had circled one of the planet's moons, that being Callisto. Recordings had been penned into folders.

The flight was all in order until a rattling sound was heard. Worried looks came across the faces of the crew. The rattling became a shudder and it was reported that one of the rockets had failed to ignite. Another rocket failed moments later and so the spacecraft was left with only one rocket to enable it to return to earth. It meant a longer and slower decent and this was communicated to Cape Canaveral. It also meant the planned re-entry into the Pacific Ocean could not be guaranteed. We all looked worried. Our food stocks were low but our drinking water was available in good supply.

We entered the Earth's atmosphere and I saw the blue Pacific Ocean disappear and be replaced by dry land. I was told we would crash land in Southern Nevada in the Mojave Desert. We all looked at each other and saw death on our faces.

The ground became larger as we descended. Oleg thought he could try a controlled crash landing and heads shook their agreement, as no one had any better solution.

Then we braced ourselves for impact. My body shook. We had reached land but our speed was still more than 500 mph. I heard branches breaking and stones hit the fuselage as we slid along the desert. Then we eventually came to a halt. We opened the hatch and realised there was a drop of twelve feet to the ground. I noticed the crash had damaged the water tank and it was spilling onto the arid land. We threw out pillows and blankets so that we could land on them but there was a rush as smoke could be detected coming from the damaged craft. It might go up in flames at any moment. We all jumped out within a minute. The American broke his ankle and was not only in pain but he could not move away from the craft. Oleg banged his head on landing and was knocked out. The other Russian stayed behind in partial shade to attend to the injured and I started to walk to get help. I had walked for four minutes when I heard a loud explosion. The spacecraft had disintegrated. I knew immediately that the two Russians and the American could not have survived that explosion.

Where was the Chinese astronaut? He was nowhere to be seen. Perhaps he was a victim too. I walked back towards the smouldering spacecraft. Then I heard the sound of an approaching helicopter. It landed and I went to board it. Another helicopter arrived and I was told it would recover the dead. I was strapped into a seat and next to me was the Chinese colleague. I thumped his knee to indicate we had survived. And I had survived. I woke shortly afterwards in a sweat.

Jean Brotherston

My name is Jean Brotherston and I was born in Dumfries.
Having left school I went to work in an office but then
changed to become a telephonist for British Telecoms.
I married, had two children Kirsty and Simon and moved
away from Dumfries for twenty years living in both
UK and abroad. I settled back in Dumfries where I took
on work as a Secretary with the NHS for 25 years until
I retired about one and a half years ago. My hobbies include
playing in a brass band (now retired), gardening, and
long walks with my friend Mo and her two dogs. I love
baking cakes (which I mostly give away), doing jigsaws (93
completed since Covid) and I am a volunteer at the River of
Life Church Foodbank three evenings a week. I also spend
as much time as I can with my 4 grandchildren, Naomi,
Kieran, James and Finlay. During Covid home schooling
definately improved my maths!

Dreams – Real

I'm not too sure where to begin – there are some types of
dreams that we have which are lovely and sweet and some
that you totally want to forget about. I am sure I may have
had some nightmares in my life but I don't wish to recall or
remember them at all, in fact I really think that I have forgotten
them already!

I recall one childhood dream that comes to mind, well
I assume it was a dream and it was so long ago I can barely
recall all the finer details.

I had a very happy childhood and cannot relate this to my
upbringing at all. Whenever I was ill or feeling unwell I always
had the same dream and it's hard to imagine now and put it
into writing. As I was lying in my bed strange things happened

and I always imagined I was 'moving on', travelling in my bed. Like flying to some strange places that were not real. Sometimes it was very dark and sometimes very light. I would be in the air travelling around the countryside, through fields and forests, by the sea and through the water. I was always on my own and don't remember ever meeting anyone. It was very strange that I always had the same dream when I was unwell.

I never have this dream now but will always remember this time of my life.

Dreams – imaginary

In later years and to this day I have imaginary dreams which I will briefly explain.

I love visiting stately homes, historic ruins and castles and while I am there I have this feeling of 'being at home'. I have visited many places such as Culzean Castle in Ayrshire, Floors Castle in the Borders, Edinburgh Castle and several in the north of Scotland. Even ruined castles in Wales and England. Also lots of famous Castles at home and Europe – too many to list. The Taj Mahal, Amber Fort in India was favourites alongside the Pyramids, Luxor and Valley of the Kings in Egypt which were just amazing. I love the history of these far-off places. However, the most memorable one and my favourite is Glamis Castle in Angus, the childhood home of the Queen Mother. When I visited all the stately rooms – Dining room, Duncan Hall and Royal apartments I was in awe of all the amazing architecture, paintings and ornaments. My imaginary dream is that I really felt 'at home' as if I had been there before. Even in the Italian and Walled gardens it was truly wonderful. I could have spent hours at Glamis dreaming of what could have been!

Rick Hale describes himself as an American author living near Illinois, a cancer survivor, an amputee, an old school ghost hunter and a Domestic God.

Hauntings At The Galleries Of Justice

For well over six centuries, in England's Nottingham, the Galleries of Justice were used to judge and jail criminals of every sort. First used by the Normans in 1375 CE as a headquarters for the Sheriff of Nottingham, made famous by the Robin Hood stories. Seventy years later in the 1440s, the building was turned into a prison. For centuries, men, women and even children were incarcerated and hanged for everything from failure to pay taxes to murder. The Normans were notorious for having very little tolerance for people who broke the law. To them, if you committed the crime be prepared to do the time. Even with your life.

Although the Galleries stopped taking prisoners decades ago, something of those old days still remains. It would appear that many of the prisoners who met their fates behind its imposing walls still lurk among the shadows. And some areas are far more haunted than others. I'll break down the areas of the Galleries where the unsuspecting visitors may just have an unforgettable brush with the inexplicable.

The Entrance Hall

The entrance Hall of the Galleries is our first stop of haunted areas. Those courageous enough to spend any amount of time in the Entrance Hall have encountered three very active phantoms. The first is a soldier who marches about the hall with a rather unpleasant scowl on his face. Before vanishing, he grunts at visitors as if he is displeased with the intrusion.

The second and third ghosts in the Entrance Hall are a kindly gentleman in Victorian era clothing. He is said to be quite friendly as he greets visitors with a smile. The third ghost is a mean old woman who, unlike the gentleman, makes it very clear that you are not welcome by yelling at people before fading away.

The Courtroom

When the Galleries of Justice were used as a court and prison, many criminals learned of their fate in the courtroom. Swift justice came down on their heads as they were either sent to dank prison cells to live out the rest of their days or had their day with the hangman at the end of a rope. Since the courtroom was the place where many met their destinies, it should come as no great surprise that it's haunted.

Guides, cleaning crew and visitors have reported various unnerving supernatural horrors in the Courtroom. Large balls of crackling lights have been witnessed zipping around the Courtroom regardless of the time of day. Large looming shadows that give off a feeling of dread and malevolence are seen lurking in the shadows. But perhaps the most unnerving activity of all is the disembodied screams for mercy by the defendants as they were dragged out of the court to their punishment.

The Chapel

The area of the Galleries of Justice that is rumoured to be the most haunted is the least likely, the Chapel. The Chapel is said to be haunted by an ill tempered ghost that tears the cross from the wall and throws it at people as they enter. Loud bangs on the wall accompanied by shrieks are heard throughout the day. And stones are thrown around the room, sometimes hitting people. Are these the spirits who begged God for forgiveness and found none? Quite possibly.

Today, the Galleries of Justice serve a much different purpose as a museum. And if your child is into the gloomy ambience of the Galleries, they can have their birthday parties among the methods of pain and torture. A bit of good macabre fun. Despite this, the Galleries of Justice do not take their spectral population lightly. The Galleries of Justice have a healthy respect for their ghosts. Even during a child's birthday party.

Miller Caldwell

ITALY in SEPTEMBER

(Night falling rain stirs dreams of an orchestra of
dripping leaves.)

A velvet green canopy over a collar of basalt rock

protects the dry crisp plain beneath

nibbled by the ink blue Mediterranean Sea.

Italy in September relaxes after the annual summer assault of
heat, of visitors and of cars.

Deep in the countryside, where silence glimpses the afterlife,
the stain of voices emerge greeting,

shuffling on sun baked grit.

The day is announced. The dancing horizon is penetrated by
hydro pylons bringing energy to fuel the day in the kitchen
and homes of a people known only by their smiles.

Descendants of Greek invaders or Roman Legionnaires, they
roam no more, content in sharing their harmony with nature,
and sun seeking northern visitors.

Night falling rain stirs dreams of an orchestra of dripping
leaves, splashing paths and roof tops

performing an impromptu drum roll.

But in the morning a calm atmosphere prevails with the
occasional drip left to descend and make its way by leaf and
branch to the vegetation beneath.

Grey clouds protect the land from a dying September
sun conserving a sharp hot moment of penetration when
least expected.

Then, and only then, swim naked in the enclosed bay
surrounded by cliffs and caves where tax free profiteering
once flourished to the sway of the cutlass and eye patch of the
Adriatic sea dog.

But now a haven, to refresh tired limbs and repel the rays of
sun striving to burn each pigment of exposed skin.

Feet tread wearily on sharp moving grit.

The nude torso fights to gain balance on land once more while
shedding sea salt drips in eyes and to the dry shore, leaving
footprints of a moment in time.

Scent the rosemary and mint in flared nostrils recalling
servings of hot roast lamb, while seeing the very same beasts
roaming the Amalfi hills oblivious to their future, and me
to mine.

Martin Greenlees is a retired special branch police officer
and has now become an author of police advice to children
in his books.

A Gas Extraction

Hi Miller

You asked about dreams and I can never remember my dreams
but here is something that may be worth exploring.

My brother tells a story of when he had gas at the dentist
while having a tooth extracted many years ago. He can recall
the grim reaper in a car ushering him into the surgery, but after
the treatment, he didn't return to the car.

I just thought the use of gas by the dentist would be of interest.

Martin

Writer **Andrew Goss** relates a haunting dream which
takes him to the distant plains of the Punjab.

A House in India

IT WAS A perfect summer's day as the sun shone through leafy,
tree-lined avenues, dappling the footpaths in patchy shade.
And the sleepy English market town was awash with the bustle
of shoppers. All dressed rather traditionally, as if they had just
stepped from a different time when England still seemed that
green and pleasant land of a different era.

The two young men, both in their late teens, stood for
a moment, slightly out of place, taking in the sights and sounds.
And to get their bearings.

"It's a big house at the end of Cedar Avenue," the first young
man repeated somewhat uncertainly to his companion. He
was taller, darker and a little older than his cousin, who stood
beside him. The scene seemed all too familiar to him, yet always
strangely elusive.

"I'm just not sure…" he added.

In his mind he knew exactly where the old house was, could
picture the way the road curved round leading to where the old
Victorian villa stood. But in reality he had to admit they were
lost. He just couldn't seem to find it.

"Perhaps we should ask someone," his cousin suggested. He
too was tall and lean, but much fairer, with a shock of light
brown hair, and piercing blue eyes, which he narrowed as he
surveyed the street scene bathed in sunshine. A casual observer
might have noted their family resemblance. It was in the eyes.

Their mission: to visit a distant, elderly and slightly eccentric
aunt, who would finally reveal the mystery that had played on
their minds increasingly this last year. She would describe the
exact nature of the family inheritance which might change their
future and, perhaps, reveal something of her own life.

But which direction to take in the hope they would come to that elusive familiar landmark? For a moment they stood watching the throng of people going about their daily business. But why was no one wearing facemasks? The whole place seemed out of step with reality.

Perhaps they should approach an older shopper, more likely to be familiar with the area. Surely someone would know where the distinctive house lay. It seemed the sort of property people would know in a town where many lived out their lives. Comfortably. Almost in isolation. The sort of place in which you met, married and settled, and families knew each other.

Yet as they contemplated their next move it was the young woman on an old-fashioned bicycle, dressed in brilliant white reflecting in the bright sunshine that captured the young men's attention. For a moment she had stopped, resting her feet on the pavement as she stood astride the contraption, leaning the cycle against her.

She glanced around uncertainly, as if she too might be lost.

Then she gazed right at the darker boy. And she smiled. Beautifully. It was a radiant and natural smile, which revealed perfect white teeth. Her eyes seemed to be smiling too and her face was framed by long blonde hair which fell upon her shoulders. In an instant, perhaps as old as creation, the young man wondered what it might be like to kiss her beautiful mouth.

"Hello," he ventured uncertainly and stepped towards her. "My cousin and I are lost. I wonder if you might help us…"

"I'll try," she replied. "But let's move away from the busy street." And she climbed from the bicycle.

In truth, she was glad of the diversion, she said. Besides, she seemed drawn to the two young men who were not unattractive to her.

"Shall we find somewhere quieter? There's a delightful tearoom in a side street just along here," she nodded towards the narrow lane which suddenly seemed to open up from the main street. And she began wheeling her cycle along as she walked towards the alleyway and the young men followed her. Away from the bustle of the main road the three found themselves at the small tearoom, where she leaned her bicycle against its frontage and they all took a place at one of the outside tables.

"I just had to get away from my writing," she told them.

"You're a writer?" said the darker young man.

"Oh yes," she replied and looked down to rummage in the small handbag which she brought to her lap. She pulled out a long 'pencil book', folded four times inwards onto the pages, which gave the narrow volume a cylindrical appearance.

"I always keep a copy with me, just in case somebody wants one," she explained. "You never know."

"I've not seen one of those before," the young man told her. And it was true, for in reality they did not exist. She handed it to him and he opened it out. Clever, he thought, as he spread the pages open and it took the size of a normal paperback.

"That's great," he said, scanning the type.

He remembered he still had a ten-pound note tucked within a corner of his own satchel.

"Is this a spare?" he asked her. "I'd very much like to have a copy."

Again she smiled the sunshine smile and nodded.

"You must tell me what you think next time we meet," she told him, as if the prospect was a certainty. And suddenly the young man felt a connection to her; that he would see her again. The feeling was warm and good and comforting, as if they might easily become friends and lovers. Already he felt he knew her; knew what it might be like to hold her. He told her he felt he had seen her before. Perhaps they had met somewhere before, he ventured?

"No," she replied. "We have never met. At least not in this world, in this life. Only in your dreams…" And she smiled faintly.

What an odd reply, he thought, suddenly feeling embarrassed and self-conscious. A deep blush burned upon his face and he felt the need to stare down at his hands. When he looked up, the young woman was gone and the two men were sitting on their own at the table.

"Can I help you?" asked the waiter.

He looked up at the face of an older man wearing an immaculate white apron, pad in hand and pencil poised to take his order.

"I'm not sure. There was a young woman with us, blonde hair, dressed in white…"

"There was no woman, sir. I saw you arrive and sit down alone," the waiter said.

And it was true. Suddenly he realised he was completely alone. His younger cousin was also gone. He was confused.

"No…erm…thank you," then pausing. "I have to go."

And the waiter smiled kindly in understanding. Must get to my cousin's house, he thought. And in an instant he was there.

***

His uncle's house lay within a leafy suburban estate on the edge of town. It was a comfortable, some might have said exclusive, neighbourhood, with well-kept gardens. The two-story four-bed property was set back from the avenue in which it lay, with flowering borders lining a sweeping driveway which led to a neatly painted door, itself framed by hanging baskets.

He rapped on the door, which opened almost immediately. And he stepped in. Inside it was extensive and smartly decorated and there was an immediate sense of order. It was a family home of people with means.

"I've been looking for you," said his cousin as he entered, "Weren't we meant to go to see Aunt Edna?"

"Yes," he replied. "Yes we were."

"Let's wait for my father. He's due any minute. And he says he has a family announcement to make…"

Uncle Edward was a precise, well-dressed man, with a small, neatly trimmed moustache. He always seemed to be dressed formally in a business suit. He wasn't sure what his uncle did as a profession, but would not have been surprised to learn he was a City banker, or company director in an insurance company. And he spoke as he dressed. Formally, with precision, but without passion.

He entered the living room as he might a boardroom, as his wife, their four children and their cousin gathered to hear his announcement, watching him expectantly.

"There is news…" said the head of the house, smoothing his moustache with his fingers. He drew a deep breath before continuing, all eyes upon him.

"Aunt Edna, sadly, is no longer with us," he announced solemnly. "She died yesterday. Peacefully, in her sleep." Again he paused.

"Yet she leaves a legacy to remember her by," he continued. There was, he told them, a magnificent estate in India, where the old lady had been raised as a girl in the days of the British Raj. And yet, she had never spoken of her time in northern Punjab, or the hot fertile plains that lay in the shadow of the Himalayas. Nor had she ever returned. There was talk of a scandal at the time. There had been a tragedy. A young woman had visited from England with her family. And she had died. No one knew the exact circumstances. Aunt Edna would never speak of it. They had been close.

She and her family had returned to England shortly afterwards, never to speak of India again. And yet the estate had remained their property, under the stewardship of a trusted foreman who oversaw the land and its tenant farmers. And the house stood there still, a magnificent colonial villa, largely boarded up and religiously kept as it had been in the final days of the Raj, in readiness for the return one day of its owners.

"So we are going to India," Uncle Edward announced, "…where we shall take up residence in the old house for several seasons and settle the estate." There was silence, as each family member considered just what it might mean.

"It is what the old girl would have wanted. She once spoke of her time there. With longing. With affection. And, I think with a sense of sadness," he added.

"And I found this among her papers," he said, pulling out an envelope from the inside pocket of his jacket. There was an old black and white photograph. The picture was faded a yellowish brown with age. Yet it had captured a happy moment in time.

Two young women in white fabric standing on the sweeping veranda, framed by majestic colonial pillars and date palms, smiling. Happy. One was a young Aunt Edna. You could see it in her eyes and the features of her face not yet marked by experience and time.

And yet it was the woman beside her with a large straw hat, whose beautiful smile was unmistakable and sent a sudden chill right through him. It was the woman with the bicycle whose sunshine smile still shone from the fading photograph taken 70 years before, gazing to camera, as if she was looking right at him. And it seemed her eyes were smiling too…

Wedding Gift

The wedding gift of an old house seems wonderful, but when other worldly events start happening, Peter and Jenny Rogers try to evict the ghost.

Peter and Jenny Rogers return from their honeymoon to a pile of wedding presents including the deed to an old house. They open presents from the residents of Whistling Pines Senior Care Center ranging from thoughtful, to thrift shop purchases, to "what is that?"

Taking a break from the gift opening party, they tune in to a live news broadcast and watch the historical society president open a time capsule found during the demolition of the band shell. The opening ceremony turns grim when a rusty pistol and a newspaper clipping about an old murder are revealed.

The Whistling Pines rumour mill runs amok as the retired residents offer up murder motives, stories about the victim's chequered past, and a multitude of potential murderers. Despite his full time job as Whistling Pines recreation director, Peter gets dragged into the time capsule murder investigation.

Jenny's son, Jeremy, is convinced their new house is haunted when boxes jump from shelves, a radio turns itself on, Christmas stockings appear under the fireplace mantle, wedding gifts rise eerily out of boxes, and ghostly events interrupt their sleep. They start to ask themselves if the house is a gift or a curse… until the ghost is revealed.

Gabriel James is an Anglo-German journalist and writer
based in the heart of England. For several years he
lived and worked in South Asia and spent time in West
Africa. *Return to Shalimar* is a work in progress. He is also
completing a further novel, set in north-east Africa.

Excerpt from Return to Shalimar

By Gabriel James alias AG

*Prelude: And the emperor commissioned the finest water gardens
to be constructed on the banks of Lake Dal for the woman he
adored, so that she might view the beauty of the moonlight from its
centre among the fragrant flowers. And the gardens were known as
Shalimar, a place of eternal happiness; a paradise on earth.*

SNOW fell from leaden skies like eiderdown feathers, floating
gently and silently onto the rolling English countryside which
stretched from his window. It was as if all the angels in heaven
were shedding their feathers, he mused, as he gazed at the
ghostly landscape outside.

The land was already white, its contours smoothed by a layer
of snow like icing on a cake. Hauntingly beautiful. And yet he
was overcome by a sense of sadness. He took a final pull on
the Ganja before tossing the charred stub into the ashtray, then
downed his Glen Fiddich. He grimaced as he felt the warm glow
run from his throat to the pit of his stomach. He could not
shake the images which had so disturbed him earlier that day.

The woman he had seen in the morning was troubled by her
past. Although he had never met her before he sensed it; felt it,
as soon as she had approached the house. Not that this was in
any way unusual. He made a living from desperate people. But
the woman who arrived that winter's day was different.

He sensed her sorrow, a hunger and desperation. He felt an overpowering sense of inevitability. He knew instantly there was a significance to her arrival. It was as if he had always known she would come. But not even he, Jack Palmer, psychic consultant, could foresee the full impact the woman's visit would have upon his own life.

"I'm sorry I'm late," she exclaimed in a voice like velvet as he opened his front door to her. Her black shoulder-length hair framed a face of classic South Asian beauty, with high, wide cheekbones whose contours swept down to a subtly cleft chin. She had an elegant, finely chiseled nose. Her lips were full and curved upwards at the corners of her mouth. And as they parted into a smile she showed immaculate white teeth whose brightness was exaggerated by her light brown complexion.

Yet beyond her youth and beauty he sensed a spirit weighed with experience spanning a thousand years.

Her dark eyes seemed to draw him in as images of sun-scorched plains of the past and exotic eastern landscapes stretching under a relentless heat swept over him. He was overcome by a sense of emotional turmoil, passion and pain.

"Come in, my dear," he said cordially. Yet his voice sounded alien to him, automatic. He was shaken. The strength of the images which radiated from her had caught him off-guard. But he quickly composed himself.

"You found me then." His mind was closing down, raising barriers against the intensity of emotion she was projecting.

"I think I took a wrong turn back there," she explained apologetically, gesturing over her shoulder. And she smiled again. She was wearing a black winter coat, jeans and a lilac linen shawl draped across her neck and shoulders.

"You'd better come in from the cold," he repeated and as he turned she followed him into the house.

"Would you like a cup of tea," he asked, smiling, having recovered from the power of the emotions which had flowed through him upon her arrival. She returned his smile and nodded.

"Thank you."

"Please take a seat," he said, inviting her to sit in one of the wooden chairs at a small breakfast table in the kitchen, then turned to put on the kettle.

"Sorry," he said, turning back to her as she sat down. "I'm Jack Palmer." And he reached forward to take her hand and clasped it in his for a moment. He had regained his composure.

"I'm Priya."

"I hope so," he chuckled and she smiled that winning smile back at him. "Nice to meet you, Priya."

He noticed she had the most beautiful hands he had ever seen, with long, slender fingers and immaculately painted nails. He had felt the energy from her hand, which he released almost reluctantly.

"Can I take your coat?"

She slipped it deftly from her shoulders, tucked her shawl into one of its sleeves and handed it to him, watching him as he hung the heavy garment onto a peg in the adjacent hallway. He was dressed casually in a chunky woolen sweater his mother might have knitted, she thought.

"Actually, if it hadn't been for the postman, I don't think I'd ever have found you," she said as he returned to the kitchen.

"I know it's not easy to find, but I wouldn't live anywhere else," he replied.

But his mind was still racing, trying to make sense of the images which were flowing from her. There was something familiar in them. Something which stirred feelings in him he could not identify, like some distant, buried memory. It was as if he knew that arid landscape; had lived and breathed the dry air and could feel its heat. And it disturbed him. There was something about the woman too. As if he had met her before. That he knew her story.

"You've not been to me before?" But even as he asked, he knew she hadn't. He would have remembered her beauty.

"No," she replied. "But you come highly recommended."

"Oh…?"

"By a friend." It was not unusual. Most of his clients came to him by personal recommendation.

"Milk and sugar?"

"Yes please. White, two sugars."

He approached with two steaming mugs of tea and placed them carefully upon coasters on the table, but he remained standing.

"I know why you're here, my dear," he said.

She said nothing, but looked quizzically into his eyes.

"You've been having dreams."

She stared at him in disbelief.

"I know," he added. "Because I've seen them too." And it was true.

He led her to a small room at the top of the house. Inside were two simple dining chairs facing each other over a small side table beneath the window, an antique cupboard and some shelving lined with books. He took a small cassette recorder from the shelf and sat opposite her, cradling it like a baby. The woman was a little nervous, but it was not in her nature to be easily frightened.

"Have you ever had a reading like this before?" he asked.

"Never," she replied. He knew it wasn't true. All her life she had been looking for answers.

"It's nothing to be scared of," he reassured her. "I'm going to tune in now." Then he lowered the lids over his china blue eyes. His face became calm and relaxed, trance-like.

He pressed the record button on the cassette player and began speaking into it as she studied him with a mixture of anxious curiosity, unable to take her eyes from his face.

"I'm seeing your dream now," he murmured. "In this dream I see a young woman dressed in flowing silks, with bangles. She is happy and she is singing… she's in love." He smiled as he felt the young woman's joy.

"She's in the privacy of her own room, but outside it is hot. The sun is low in the clear blue sky, full and red. The heat of the day is giving way to the soothing evening shadows stretching across the dusty streets of a city of bleached, flat-roofed houses… and she is happy as the night is approaching. I see a city surrounded by water, set against mountains that rise majestically to meet the sky."

He paused and opened his eyes. "Do you recognize this place, Priya?"

She hesitated. "It's a place I've been dreaming of," she finally replied in a voice that was trembling. He closed his eyes and continued.

I see a man. He is the man she adores. They are lovers." He paused again. "Such passion." And he smiled as he felt the intensity of their emotion run through him.

"What does he look like?" she whispered.

"He's dark and handsome, with clean features and high cheekbones. He wears a head cloth, a turban… like an Arab prince… and there is life and warmth in his eyes. She loves the life that dances in his eyes."

It was the same man she herself had dreamed of. A man she felt incredibly drawn to, like a hunger that could not be satisfied, or a thirst that would not be quenched, she longed for him. But always with sadness.

"Do you know him?"

Again she felt his eyes upon her. She shook her head. "Who is he?" she asked.

"He seems to be… hmmm… a man of status. He rides a white stallion, wears fine clothes and jewellery. I see him as a leader of men." He broke off.

"But there is treachery everywhere. There is a need for secrecy. Theirs is a forbidden love. There is envy, jealousy and betrayal surrounding their happiness in those who would seek to destroy it."

"Who?" Her voice was barely audible.

"I don't know," he said blankly. "I can't see."

Suddenly he opened his eyes and gazed right at her.

"Does this make any sense to you, Priya?"

"It's the dream I've been having," she told him. And he closed his eyes again.

"This is what I see. But you don't recognize the man?"

"Only from my dreams. But it feels like I *know* him…" She hesitated. "That I love him…"

"Like the girl with the bangles."

"Yes! Like the woman in my dream."

"I can see it…" He stopped.

"What does it all mean?" she asked.

"I'm not sure," he replied. "But I know you will meet this man and when you do, you'll recognise him."

"This is crazy," she said.

"It's what I see," he insisted.

"Are you telling me the man I am dreaming about actually exists?"

"I think he does. I think this is what your dream is telling you…"

"How? How will I recognise him?"

"You'll know." He was frowning in an effort to see more, but the images were slipping from him.

"I'm asking for answers, but they are not coming. They are hidden," he told her. "It's fading…" But it was a lie. He had not told her everything. What was coming to him didn't make sense. She was the woman in the vision he saw.

"You are going to meet this man soon. And when you do, it will seem as if you have been sleeping. This man will awaken all your love. He will make you feel complete, as if you've been waiting for him all your life."

As he opened his eyes he smiled right at her. She lowered her eyelids, which fluttered nervously under the sudden intensity of his gaze. It was an affliction she had when she became nervous, which lent her an air of vulnerability. Her heart was beating fast as she felt the passion she had seen and *felt* in her dreams.

"Can you tell me more?" she asked.

"I can't, my dear. Not today. The rest will show itself in a matter of weeks."

He closed his eyes again. "I'm looking into your life now…" He began to describe the people she worked with at the office.

"It's some kind of legal work…"

"I'm a solicitor," she told him.

"But you won't be working there too much longer." He paused. "Have you got an idea to work for yourself?"

"I suppose I have," she replied. "I'd like to make and sell my own jewellery."

"That's what I see. You could be successful selling your own work… you're very creative, you know. Great business sense and an ability to make money. And you're good with people. They are drawn to you. But there's more… you'll be travelling overseas."

In many respects hers had been an ordinary life. But that was about to change. And he saw she had a troubled past. She had known disappointments in love and had led a life that was unfulfilled. He saw too that she had overcome an unhappy childhood that had left her craving attention and affection. Despite her outward confidence she was desperately insecure from a difficult relationship with her father. She had so wanted to be loved; had felt rejected by a man who always seemed to have time for everyone else, except her. He felt the pain and frustration of her relationships with men.

"He did love you in his own way," he told her. "But he wasn't able to show it in the way you needed to be loved." And she had cried. He saw too she had resented him for what he had done to her mother. It had coloured her own relationships with men, so that she had grown up with the anger of rejection in her heart. She had found it hard to love. Yet he knew the man she was to meet would change all that. But he did not tell her everything he had seen. It was too much. And he was getting tired.

"I've told you all I can for today," he said. "I'm going to shut down now." The images of her dreams were still strong in his mind. But he did not say so.

"Follow your heart, your instincts… your dreams," he told her.

"I'm not sure I know how," she replied.

"It will make sense as time goes by," he promised. "What's

happening to you is positive. It is something meant to be. It is your destiny," he continued.

"What must I do?" she asked in a voice thick with emotion.

"Follow your intuition, which is good. Your heart will guide you." He drew a deep breath. "That's all I'm getting. I hope what I have told you makes sense," he said finally and she nodded.

"I promise you, this is something exciting coming your way which will change your life for the better. Let me know how things go. And I hope you come and see me again." He knew she would.

Then she left him. He watched her walk to her car as the first snow began to fall. She turned towards him as she climbed in. What a strange day, she thought, waving to him as she drove away.

After she had gone he lifted his eyes to the heavens, watching the snowflakes drifting through the grey sky. Then he turned and went inside. He felt drained. She had been the first to find him. But there would be others. Each drawn together by a destiny demanding to be fulfilled. He felt the time was approaching.

Later, as his eyes rested on the white slopes outside, he saw them melt into the desert dunes once more. The same scene was unfolding before him he had felt in the young woman's presence. What he hadn't told her was that hers was the same recurring dream which he himself had been haunted by. The same lovers, the same setting, but from a different perspective. While she felt overwhelming love and desire, his feeling was one of unhappiness. He tried to shake it.

She was certainly a fascinating woman with an interesting past. Destiny had brought her to him. But he was disturbed by what he had seen and what he felt. More dreams would come. He also knew he would see her again soon. What he did not know yet was that their lives were to become intertwined in a way which would change their future forever.

Miller Caldwell provides a dream based on reality during Christmas 1962.

Through the Eyes of The Blind

In alternative years my younger cousins and their parents came from Scotstoun in the west end of Glasgow to the Shawlands Old Parish Church manse on Boxing Day. I was aged 12, my sister 14 and my three Glasgow west end cousins were, blind Brian aged 10, Dorothy 8, and Douglas 6. All the children sat near a roaring fire.

Midway through the afternoon, my father announced he had to fulfil an engagement at the Victoria Hospital, where he was the chaplain. I knew the plan was afoot. He waved goodbye to us all. My older sister was in on the secret too and we were told not to inform our cousins. Accordingly, it was no surprise to us that half an hour later we heard bells. Santa's reindeers were arriving at the manse. The younger children were besides their selves in excitement as they heard Santa coming upstairs to the lounge. The door opened and sure enough Santa Claus appeared in his red and white attire, black boots and a white beard to be proud to wear, and be disguised. He arrived with a large brown sack over his shoulder.

Santa checked he was at the right house by asking each child their name. Dorothy informed Santa that her older brother was blind but he was hearing every word.

Santa read each child's name and Dorothy, Joan, Douglas and I came to Santa and received our Christmas presents.

'Now that leaves just one present left. There's only one parcel left in my sack.' Santa lifted it out and asked, 'It's for Brian. Now where is Brian?'

Dorothy led her blind brother to Santa and he received his present. However, polite Brian just had to give his thanks.

'Thank you Uncle Jim,' he said.

'No, no that's Santa, Brian. Not Uncle Jim,' explained Dorothy immediately and with concern not to offend Santa.

Brian took on board what Dorothy had said. But before returning to his place by the fire, he spoke once more to Santa.

'Thank you, Uncle Jim, for my present.'

Rozalia Aleksandrova – Representing Bulgaria

Rozalia Aleksandrova lives in Plovdiv, Bulgaria. She was born in the magical Rhodope Mountains, the cradle of Orpheus. She is a lecturer in Bulgarian language to foreign students at the Medical University, Plovdiv. Author of 11 poetry books: *The House of My Soul* (2000), *Shining Body* (2003), *The Mystery of the Road* (2005), *The Eyes of the Wind* (2007) , Parable of the key (2008), *The Conversation between Pigeons* (2010), *Sacral* (2013), *The Real Life of Feelings* (2015), *Pomegranate from Narrow* (2016), *Brushy* (2017), and *Everything I did not say* (2019). Rozalia has poetic books with selected poems translated into Polish – at the Royal Library in London, 2015. She is the editor and compiler of over ten literary almanacs, collections and anthologies. She is a member of the Union of Bulgarian Writers. In March 2006 she created a poetic-intellectual association "Quantum and Friends" for the promotion of quantum poetry in civil society, Plovdiv and Bulgarian phenomenon. Initiator and organizer of the International Festival of Poetry SPIRITUALITY WITHOUT BORDERS from 2015.

I GIFT YOU

I gift you generosity of time.
And I flow away into the ocean,
Into the lavish sunrise of words,
And the quiet sunset in Hosanna.
With which I follow your soul.
With which I run to the Hill.
And thorns and sand rinse.
I do not stop
on the way to the steep.
The crown of my vigil
is your cheerful caress.
And every bright insight
is
a blessing
from a heavenly kiss.

Gurpreet Dhariwal is the author of *My Soul Rants: Poems of a Born Spectator*. Her first poetry book got her appreciation and accolades from people all over the world. She has done her double masters in Information Technology and Computer Applications. She found her bliss in writing when she was 18 years old. She firmly believes in karma philosophy and humanity.

Her poetry reflects the poignant situations that are neglected at large. Her artwork appears as well. She can be read at:

https://medium.com/@dhariwalgurpreet

Dreaming of A New World

I am dreaming of a new world,
Where nobody would be cursed,
Killed, mocked, and betrayed.

I am dreaming of a new world,
Where nobody would be harassed,
Mentally, emotionally and physically.

I am dreaming of a new world,
Where nobody would be a slave,
Up above or beneath the grave.

I am dreaming of a new world,
Where nobody would be strangulated,
Murdered, trampled, and smashed.

John Coster is a Journalist, Educator and Documentarian at the Doc.Media Centre in Leicester.

One More Day

I do have a dream that comes and goes… I know I'm awake but cannot see… it's dark and cold. I sense someone close by. I know if I do nothing it's over. I have to move forward. Come with me, I say into the blackness. As I move I sense more following. We move forward and feel the gradient going upwards. I've no vision so can't see what I'm fighting but as I get more and more tired, I collect more and more people. Their outlines start to appear as it gets lighter and then we turn a corner. There it is. The light. I feel the breeze and smell the clean air. It's warm. I sense the danger behind us in the dark and head for the light. One more step. I'm awake. The same dream? I'm asked. Yes. What does it mean?

The people I'm leading out of the dark will be the faces I've seen over the years... I wake exhausted as though it really happened. Well I guess it did… the day before and the day before that and of course the coming day.

One more day.

One Christmas Eve

Kevin McCann

A Sherlock Holmes Story....

The build up to Christmas had been (as it was every year) a tense time. As I've recorded elsewhere Holmes found the Festive season difficult; but then Holmes found all outpourings of emotion difficult. He was not a completely cold calculating machine (though it often suited his purpose to be thought of as one); on the contrary, he was a man of deep feelings that on more than one occasion threatened to overwhelm him. Hence the cocaine binges, the bouts of listless melancholy and the exceptionally disputatious nature.

One learned to ask his opinion first before venturing one's own and then (for the sake of peace) quietly agreeing; so it was that this particular Christmas Eve I had just finished A Christmas Carol and as I closed the book with a satisfied sigh, Holmes looked up from the fire and said, "So, Watson, are you a believer in ghosts and spirits?"

"No," I responded with a smile, "but I do believe they make for good stories." Too late! I remembered that I should have asked Holmes for his "expert opinion" before venturing one of my own. The warning signs were all there. He was smoking his old black clay pipe. He'd been largely silent for the week running up to Christmas.

Holmes smiled. "A very neatly turned phrase; you should write that down, Watson."

I limited myself to, "Thank you, Holmes."

"However," he added, "I do know of at least one incident which defies rational explanation. Would you care to hear it?" He paused. "And I do assure you, my dear fellow, that everything I tell you for the next quarter hour will be the absolute truth." I glanced up at the clock; it was just fifteen minutes shy of

Midnight. "Your blanket dismissal of the supernatural surprises me, Watson," he continued. "A man of science should approach the seemingly inexplicable with an open mind."

"Open certainly," I responded rather warmly, "but not gullible surely?"

Holmes eyed me coldly. "Would you say Sir Oliver Lodge was a gullible man?"

"Well no…"

"Even though he's set up the Society for Psychical Research whose sole aim is to investigate the supernatural?"

I could see that he was spoiling for a fight and I was in no mood. *Just agree,* I thought, *it's easier…*but I must also acknowledge that my Christmas Eve reading had been lubricated with a fair amount of whisky and water and was disinclined to simply roll over submissively. "And in thirteen years have they uncovered anything other than sleight of hand and wishful thinking? I think I may have already lost count of the fraudulent mediums they have managed to expose already."

"Early days yet, my dear fellow."

The temptation to cap this with, "And they won't either!" was strong but it was late, I was tired and as I said before, it was easier just to agree. I refilled my glass and then said, "Very well, Holmes, I'm listening." Before adding with a smirk, "Include every detail no matter how trivial." I took another sip of my drink and sat back. The truth of it is I enjoyed listening to Holmes' talk. I've noted elsewhere his acting abilities and they weren't just his gift of seeming to become the person he was disguised as; it was his voice which could hold me enthralled in just the same way his violin playing did. Once caught in his spell, the world faded and time passed elsewhere.

Holmes smiled and drew deeply on his pipe. It had gone out so there was a lengthy pause whilst he refilled it, lit it with a coal from the fire held in the tongs, took several long drafts then sat back in his chair, steepled his fingers and began, "I went up to Oxford in '72 and that Christmas returned to our family farm in North Lancashire. It was a long and difficult journey which

I broke with an overnight stay in Crewe before continuing north as far as Lancaster. From there I had to change again for the branch line to our local station. The last part of the journey was in many ways the worst. The carriage was freezing, the hard bench seats profoundly uncomfortable and as it was now dark, the view from the window was universal blackness as the moon was yet to rise. I don't know whether you are familiar with the geology and topography of North Yorkshire, Watson but I can tell you it is in its own way quite beautiful and reminds me of the landscape of Ireland. However I digress; when I finally arrived at Wightwell Halt I was tired, cold and hungry. I was met by our housekeeper's son Tadgh who then drove me back up to the family farm. Truth to tell, I was glad to see him. He had been (when I was younger) much more than a mere servant. He had been both friend and mentor and a great comfort to me when my mother died."

I'd noticed the hesitation when he was telling me this last and my heart went out to him. I too knew that pain of loss and was about to say something but then thought better of it. Holmes' face assumed an expression of such grief and sorrow that any words I uttered would sound hollow. A full minute must have passed before Holmes seemed to come back to himself and continue his narrative.

"It was just past ten of the clock when I finally arrived. My two older brothers…"

"You have two brothers?" I interrupted. I knew of course about Mycroft. We had met during the case I was later to write up as the *Greek Interpreter*.

I could see Holmes wanted to ignore the question. "Yes, Watson, I have two older brothers. Mycroft, as you know, occupies a position in the Treasury. My other brother Sherrinford is…" and here his voice trailed off. This was a trait in Holmes' character I'd noted before. He would sometimes pause in mid-sentence, eyes glassy, every gesture frozen and then suddenly continue as if nothing had happened. "My two older brothers were spending Christmas with friends. Father had been constantly drunk ever since our Mother had died some years ago...actually died at Christmas so...so there was no festive welcome awaiting me." And here he paused again.

I took a sip of my whisky and waited silently whilst he composed himself. The revelation in regard to his mother's death explained a great deal.

"I had (of course) gone in to see Father as soon as I arrived home," Holmes continued, "and found (to no great surprise) that he was already several sheets to the wind. He was civil enough and asked me how I was enjoying Oxford, if I was fine for cash and so on, but he was clearly distracted. It had been drizzling when I arrived and at one point a gust of wind threw some rain against his study window. His reaction was startling. He pulled a service revolver from his desk drawer, threw himself down full length onto the floor whilst shrieking, 'Get down, you fool!' and then crawled under his desk. To some, I suppose, it might have appeared comic."

Again, I nodded silently. I'd seen similar displays during my time in hospital whilst recovering from the wound I picked up at Maiwand. As if reading my mind, Holmes said, "You'll no doubt be familiar with this mode of behaviour, Doctor?"

"Sadly, yes," I concurred. "It shames me to say," I added, "that some Army Medicos simply dismiss it as plain cowardice."

Holmes paused again to re-light his pipe before continuing, "As it shames me to admit that at the time I put it down to the blue devils that haunt the dreams of lunatics and drunkards. I even humoured him by crawling on my hands and knees across the room and cautiously peering out of the window. As I began standing up I heard him hiss frantically 'Stay down you fool!' I turned to him and said in the calmest tone I could muster, 'It's all right, Father. There's nothing there.' Well the long and short of it is that after several more minutes of quiet reason I finally persuaded him to come out. To my amazement he sat back in his chair and said, 'You must be hungry after your long journey. Ask Maeve to get you a bit of supper.'

I was tempted to interrupt and point out that sudden swings of mood are not uncommon in cases like this but I was anxious to hear the rest of Holmes' narrative and only vaguely aware of our clock chiming the hour as he continued, "So I bid him goodnight and made my way to the kitchen where Maeve our housekeeper was already putting up a very decent supper for me. Tadgh was already sat at the table. I noted that both he and his Mother were tense and when I asked why, Maeve told me the whole district was in an uproar. A good many sheep had been killed and it was thought a wild dog was responsible. 'It only started a month ago,' she went on, 'but we've lost sheep and so has every farmer round here.' Tadgh nodded and then added, 'We've had men out at night keeping watch but whatever it is, it's crafty. Old Mister Rimmer even put out some poisoned meat but all he managed to kill was a young fox barely half grown. Two nights later he lost the rest of his sheep and one of his dairy cows.' Here he paused. Finished him. Three days later we found him dead. Hung himself.' 'No paw prints?' I said. 'No scent for our dogs to follow?'

Tadgh shook his head, 'Nothing.'

Maeve put her hand gently on his forearm, 'Tell him the rest.'

Tadgh glared down at the table top and I could see he was under some terrible strain. 'It's trivial, Ma and besides which…'

That was as far as he got. 'Ah come on now son, you know better than that. Nothing's trivial. Now tell him!'

He turned to me, 'The dogs won't track. Whenever we've taken them to the places where it's happened, they turn tail and run as soon as we let them off the leads.'

Now this puzzled me. These were not pampered Peeks, they were working dogs. 'Have any travelling menageries been through the area?'

'No,' Tadgh shook his head. 'Nor any gypsies with dancing bears neither.'

'I cut a cob of farm cheese, bit off a large chunk and washed it down with some ale whilst I pondered. 'And nobody has seen anything?' Again Tadgh shook his head. I was baffled. A fox or a dog would have left some physical evidence: paw prints etc.

and a trail our farm dogs could follow. That was always the way of it in the past. These were deep waters indeed; but it was late and I was extremely tired so I bid them both goodnight and retired to my old bedroom at the top of the house.

Next morning over breakfast Maeve told me it had happened again and on our land too. 'Tadgh and some of the other hands are already up there, though what good it'll do…' She trailed off and I noted her hands were trembling.

So despite her protests, I skipped breakfast and made my way up to the lower meadow. It was a grim sight. Half a dozen sheep, their bodies oddly shrunken, were scattered around. I stepped cautiously into the meadow and began scanning the ground in the hope of finding at least a paw print. I found nothing. I'd also noted that all the dead sheep had had their throats torn out, but there was no little or no blood on the ground. Given the nature of their injuries the ground should have been drenched so obviously their wounds had been inflicted post-mortem.

The farm dogs were all cowering by the gate refusing now to even enter the meadow let alone pick up and track a scent. A cart arrived and as the farmhands began loading the corpses onto the back of it, I circled the meadow in the hope of finding further clues. I reached the stone wall that edged it, climbed over and continued looking around. There were no prints, human or animal, of any kind.

I decided there was nothing further to be learned here and went back home for breakfast. To my surprise my father was in the kitchen talking to Maeve when I got back. To my even greater surprise he was sober. 'You've seen,' he began.

'Yes,' I replied. 'Any thoughts?' he asked.

'Not yet,' I replied.

He nodded, 'Quite right. We must begin with what we know…which is very little admittedly…and proceed from there. So what do we know?'

I held up my left hand and marked off points on my fingers. 'Livestock is being killed and then mutilated post-mortem.'

'He raised an eyebrow, 'You know this how?'

'Lack of blood on the ground; I haven't checked but I'm assuming it's been the case with all the other attacks.' He nodded so I went on. 'Whatever it is leaves neither tracks nor trail of any kind and our farm dogs not only refuse to cast around for a scent, they appear terrified.'

'Which tells us?'

'Which tells us,' I went on, 'that it's something outside their or our usual experience. And whatever it is seems to kill for pleasure. The dead sheep were mutilated but uneaten. Now that's the usual pattern with foxes and feral dogs but if it were a fox or a feral dog our farm dogs would not be afraid to track it.'

'Could it be a big cat of some kind?'

I shook my head. 'A big cat would eat its kill.'

Father actually smiled. 'Some of the locals believe it's Black Shuck.'

I suppressed a laugh. 'The Hound of Hell you mean...?' and here I glanced at Maeve whom I noted crossed herself so reigned in my urge to ridicule. 'And you?'

He merely shook his head and said, 'Come with me.'

I followed him through the house into his study. I noted he'd cleared away his desk top and there was a large map spread out on it. He turned to me. 'This is a large scale map of the area. Now look,' he said pointing to a series of red crosses that dotted its surface. 'Each one of those represents an attack by whatever it is that's killing our sheep and cattle. Do you notice anything?'

I looked down. 'If you were to connect them they would form a rough circle.'

'Oval,' he corrected me. 'Now there have been five attacks including last night's and each has taken place roughly fourteen days after the previous one; so no correlation between the attacks and the phases of the moon...which tells us?'

'We're not dealing with either a real lunatic or a mythical werewolf.' I paused as a thought struck me. 'If it was either carrying off or eating one of its kills I would incline to the theory that it's some kind of predator that gorges itself and then need not feed again for about two weeks.'

'But…'

'It doesn't eat its kills, which makes me incline towards the idea that it is human and is either some kind of sadist or someone who has a grudge against the farmers whose livestock he's killed.'

'And yet leaves no footprints or physical, traces of any kind at the scenes of slaughter.'

I sat down opposite him, accepted a cigar, lit it and then went on, 'Difficult but not impossible. Were the ewes examined for signs of sexual molestation?'

Father nodded, 'In every case but we found nothing.'

I looked again at the map and noticed Wightwell Woods was close to the scene of the first attack. It was on land adjacent to ours owned by a Major Rothwell. There were rumours that it was haunted but most people believed they had begun being circulated by the Major to discourage trespassers in very much the way smugglers encouraged the belief in phantom horsemen; and for much the same reason.

Father clearly noticed I was looking at Wightwell Woods. 'That map's out of date,' he said. 'Rothwell's had over half of the trees felled. They're old oaks mainly and I'm told the timber will fetch a good price; but the woods itself is little more than a copse so nowhere to hide in there.'

I glanced across at him. 'Has anybody checked?'

'No,' he said, 'Old Rothwell tends to shoot trespassers on sight and besides which, it would be a waste of time; a fool's errand.'

I, however, was not convinced so later that morning made my way to Wightwell Woods. As I stepped into what was left of the trees the skin on my face and hands tightened with the sudden cold. The remaining trees were leafless and it was silent. Not a single rookery or single rook was to be found there.

There was a path of sorts that led me to what I assumed was more or less the centre and an old well, its stonework scabbed with lichen. I peered over the edge and dropped a pebble in. I counted the seconds before hearing the faint splash of it hitting bottom so I calculated the well to be approximately thirty feet deep. I doubted very much that anything could climb back out of that once it was in. I picked up another pebble, peered over the edge and watched it fall into the darkness. I waited for the second splash. It never came; or at least I never heard it.

I felt compelled to lean a little further over, peering into the dark and as I dropped a third pebble, a much larger one this time, part of the well's lip crumbled underneath me and I just managed to throw myself backwards in time. As I lay there I heard loud splashes as the dislodged chunks of stone hit bottom.

Now it is an oddity in human nature than when we have had a brush with death, we are often not exhilarated at our lucky escape but haunted by the images of what so very nearly happened. So it was with me. I lay there fighting to breathe and looking up at a rapidly darkening sky. Black clouds that promised hail were rushing in to cover the sun's face and what had been a barely noticeable breeze was already growing in strength. I rolled onto my side, pushed myself up into a kneeling position and tried to stand. After three attempts I finally managed and stumbled back the way I'd come; and the whole time I could see myself falling into that darkness as clearly as I now see you, Watson.

I arrived at our farm breathless and sweating ice-water. I found Maeve in the kitchen, blurted out my story then fainted. I came to, propped up on a settle in front of the fire. Maeve and Tadgh were both looking concerned and they'd been joined by my father. I was surprised to note that despite the fact it was now late afternoon, he was still sober.

After I'd repeated my story he berated me for going off on my own without telling anybody, trespassing on Rothwell's land, damaging his property and nearly getting myself killed. He finished with, 'And for all that did you find anything apart from an old well?' I shook my head. 'Still, no real harm done I suppose and we can eliminate the woods as a possible hiding place for our mysterious killer...unless of course it lives down the well.'

I shrugged. 'Impossible; nothing could get in and out of that.' But even as I spoke I was haunted by the thought that I'd missed something obvious. I was startled out of my reverie by an enfilade of hail that swept across the farmyard and ricocheted off the windows and roof.

Unusually Father joined me for my evening meal and even more unusually drank nothing stronger than water. We ate in silence. Outside the hail had turned to heavy rain and there was a bitterly cold west wind riding in on its back. Once we'd finished eating I excused myself and retired to my room. It had been a long day and I was tired. The moon was on the wane but there was enough light for me to make out the hedgerow bordering an adjacent lane. Everything looked normal and the hedge swayed like a long ship riding at anchor except for one thin tall section that remained perfectly still.

I slept deeply and awoke to a bright sunny morning. The storm had burned itself out and there was a clear sky. I went to open the window to let in some much desired fresh air when I noted what looked like finger-marks: five of them, spaced unusually widely apart and on the outside of the glass window. At first I thought I must be mistaken and that they were on the inside so rubbed at one of them with my index finger but it made no difference.

I raised the window just enough to lean out and look down. My bedroom was at the very top of the house so it was a fair drop to the farmyard below. The wall itself was craggy in places and ivy grew over it in abundance so it was not impossible that someone could have climbed up in the night and peered in. The thought made me shudder. I was put in mind of that certain young man that Magwitch conjured to terrify Pip.

I confess I was badly shaken and it obviously showed. As I sat down to breakfast both Maeve and my Father (still sober) commented on my pallor and both were obviously relieved when I did full justice to my breakfast. Tadgh came in just as I was finishing and reported that he'd been out since sunrise and found no evidence of further attacks.

Maeve was bustling about and complaining loudly about *folk underfoot;* Father, Tadgh and I took the hint and adjourned to the parlour. It was then I told them about the finger-marks. I ended with, 'I didn't want to say anything in front of Maeve as I had no wish to alarm her.'

Father nodded. 'Quite right.' Then suggested we go up to my bedroom so he could see for himself. Tadgh came with us and after we'd satisfied ourselves that they really were finger-marks, Father turned to me and said, 'Do you remember anything else? Think hard; anything no matter how trivial.'

I told them about the unmoving part of the hedge and was about to say, 'But that's all,' when something else came back to me. I'd either been awoken or dreamt I was awoken by a tapping on my bedroom windowpane and when I looked I saw it was a moth.

Father and Tadgh exchanged a glance and then he said, 'Describe it.'

I was puzzled, 'It was just a moth.'

'Humour me; describe it in as much detail as you can.'

'It was either black or deep blue, seemed a little larger than is usual and its eyes must have been reflective as they shone red in the candlelight.' But even as I said it, I realised my error. In reality the candle was extinguished so I must have been dreaming; but when I put this to Father he merely said, 'Perhaps,' before adding, 'How much do you remember about our travels in Europe?'

'I should tell you, Watson, that during my early childhood we were nomads and travelled extensively around Europe. It had not been a uniformly happy time.' I hesitated before finally answering. 'I remember endless dreary inns, bad food and damp sheets. I remember travelling in the coach and Mother helping to pass the time by telling us stories.'

Father nodded. 'She would collect them the way some people collect paintings.'

I cut across him, 'I remember her telling us the story of Bluebeard…'

He held up his hand to silence me. 'If I may be allowed to continue; she became convinced that certain stories were faint echoes of real events. At the time I naturally resisted all attempts she made to convince me but now…well now I'm not so sure. Tell me again about your visit to Wightwell Woods. Omit nothing no matter how apparently trivial.'

So I told him again and when I came to the part concerning the well I mentioned that when I dropped the second pebble I hadn't heard a splash.

'You're sure of that?' he asked quietly.

'Certain,' I replied.

'Continue.' I finished my story. He sat in silence and then said, 'Why did you lean over? Think carefully.'

'I was about to say, 'To get a better look', when I realised that wasn't true. 'I felt compelled.'

'You're sure about that?'

I nodded and noticed that Father and Tadgh exchanged another glance and then he said, 'Are you game to go back? Not alone I might add.' Again, I nodded. 'Good man! A mention in dispatches I think.' Then he turned to Tadgh. 'Round up as many of the farmhands as can be spared. Issue them with shotguns. Don't bother with the dogs. One last thing; you're a Catholic aren't you?'

'I am, Sir.'

'Does either you or your mother own a crucifix?'

'We both do, Sir.'

'Bring it with you and a good length of stout rope about.' And here he turned to me. 'You said the well is about thirty feet deep?' I nodded and he turned back to Tadgh. 'About thirty feet in length. Do we have such an item?'

And with a 'We do' Tadgh turned smartly on his heel and went downstairs. Father then turned back to me. 'I confess I do have some misgivings about taking you along with us. There may be an element of danger.'

Tadgh had rounded up half a dozen farmhands so counting Father, Tadgh and myself, we were nine strong. I mentioned this to Tadgh as we approached Wightwell Woods and he smiled saying, 'Triple three; good number.' And then refused to say any more.

When we arrived at what was now little more than a copse, Father gathered the men around him. 'I think that whatever has been killing livestock may be hiding in there; possibly in a disused well. If I'm right, it is nothing natural. Make sure your shotguns are loaded and if I give the order to fire do so without hesitation. Your lives may depend on it.'

The hands exchanged uneasy glances and there were distinct mutterings of 'Not paying us enough for this!' Father waited for silence. 'Any man who wishes to go back to the farm is free to do so. Nobody will think any the less of you.' He paused. Nobody moved. 'Very well; stay close together, no more than an arm's length between each man. Tadgh, my son and myself will lead; you follow not more than three paces behind.'

As we stepped into the trees I noted again the sudden cold. The others did too. It was an odd kind of cold in that it seemed to come from within; a cold that began in your bones. We moved silently and cautiously forward until reaching the clearing then Father gave whispered commands to the men who, at a distance of no more than a yard, encircled the well.

It was now considerably colder; so cold we could see our own breath pluming in the darkening air. I glanced up and through a gap in the trees saw black clouds pouring across the sky. What had begun as a bright sunny morning was rapidly transforming itself into a dark and stormy night. A strong wind began prowling the outskirts of the clearing whipping dead leaves up into swirling columns. I could see the farmhands were about ready to cut and run but, as both Tadgh and Father appeared calm, they stayed in position.

Father instructed Tadgh to tie the crucifix to one end of the rope and then begin slowly lowering it down the well. He then beckoned me over and said, 'I need you to act as look out.' And here he cocked his loaded pistol and pointed it down the well. 'Your eyes are younger than mine. If you see anything moving down there, point it out to me and then get back with the others.' He then turned back to the hands. 'If anything comes out of that well, give Tadgh, my son and myself enough time to lie flat and then open fire. Remember, it eats therefore it has a body and the concentrated fire power of six shotguns at that close range will disintegrate it. By all means pray to the Holy Virgin but shoot to kill.'

He then turned back to Tadgh and myself. 'Ready?' We both nodded and as Tadgh began lowering the crucifix into the dark, I peered over the rim whilst Father stood opposite me. All I could see was darkness but then just for a moment I could swear there were two red lights about the size of farthings gleaming back up at me.

'There Father,' I shouted, pointing, and as he emptied his pistol down the well, Tadgh was jerked forward as something on the other end pulled on the rope with such tremendous force it ran though his hands and left him (we later discovered) with palms skinned and blistered. At that exact moment, what was left of the daylight was completely blotted out. My ears were still ringing from Father's pistol shots and I was deafened as well as blind. I felt an explosive force that threw me backwards. This was followed by a terrible stench that clogged my nostrils and left me gagging.

I became slowly aware of a hand on my shoulder and light in the clearing again. I looked up and saw Father mouthing something at me which I was finally able to make out as, 'Are you all right?' I nodded and got slowly onto my feet. Tadgh was also getting back up after obviously being thrown back too.

Father pushed part of the stonework (which was now bellied out and widely cracked) down the well then turned to the farmhands who also appeared to have been knocked flat and were now getting unsteadily to their feet. 'We need to seal this up. Start by pushing in the remainder of the stonework and then anything you can lay your hands on.' He must have noticed their hesitancy because he then added, 'Don't worry. The sight of the holy cross paralysed it while I put six bullets into it at almost point blank range. It's dead so let's bury it.'

And so we did; we pushed the remaining stonework down the well and followed up with as much dead wood (and there was a fair bit) as we could gather. It was late afternoon and getting on for dusk by the time we'd finished and began making our way back home. We were all tired but in surprisingly high spirits. Father had given a little speech just before we set off. He told the hands that he was proud of them, suggested we put about a story that our sheep killer was a large dog we'd tracked and shot then presented each of them with a guinea.

By the time we arrived home we were all tired. Father and myself both washed and changed into fresh linen and then sat down at the kitchen table and did full justice to the meal Maeve had prepared. We were joined by Tadgh and all three of us ate more or less in silence. I noted Father took ale with his meal (as did Tadgh and myself) but only drank moderately. After we'd eaten we adjourned to the parlour (Tadgh as well) and Father and I smoked cigars whilst Tadgh stuck to his clay pipe. A companiable silence grew between us which I finally broke with, 'What was it?'

Father flicked the ash off his cigar into the fireplace and said, 'There's no one name for its kind. In India they're called the Baital. In Ireland the Dearg-due.' Here he glanced across at Tadgh who nodded and then turned back to me. 'And in Hungary the Nosferatu. That's where your mother first heard of them. I'd already heard stories whilst I was serving in India but dismissed them as native superstition. It was the same during my time in Ireland but then after I left the army and we were travelling in Europe your mother began collecting tales about them. She told me the signs to look out for: animals killed and drained of blood; the ability of these things to change shape and become bats or moths; the fact that they always have a nest in the earth and are destroyed by religious talismans such as a cross. You were partly correct about the dead sheep. Their throats were torn out post mortem but they were killed by being drained of blood. The mutilations were designed to hide that fact.'

'And there was more, Watson, a great deal more.' At one point Father produced a bottle of brandy and three glasses. I noted that both he and Tadgh only took small measures but the one he poured for me was…generous. I sat and listened in fascination as both he and Tadgh regaled me with stories of these creatures. Time wore on and eventually sleep overwhelmed me. I vaguely recall being led by Father and supported by Tadgh into my bedroom and being laid down to sleep. I heard Father say (as if from a long way off), 'Goodnight, my boy. Sleep well. Sweet dreams.'

My dreams however were far from sweet. I dreamed I was being pursued across open country by a dark thin shape until I eventually reached home and climbed into the apparent safety of my bed. There was a full moon and my bedroom curtains were open. I saw a clawed hand reach in through the gap between the partly raised window and the sill, raise the window even further and then a thin figure clad only in a few rags slid over the sill, dropped down on all fours and began snuffling like a dog.

I could feel a scream gathering at the back of my throat and when it finally escaped came fully awake, sat up in bed and saw the figure from my dream crouched as if about to pounce. The moon, as I said, was full and as it raised its head I could see a face that was more bone than flesh, mouth open in a lipless grin to reveal long canine teeth and red eyes glinting in bony sockets.

It began moving slowly across the floor towards me. I tried to move, to scream again, but it was as if I was bound and gagged. The room was now icily cold and I could see my own breath clouding in front of me. I wanted to look away, to close my eyes but I was like a rabbit in the thrall of a snake. It half rose and opened its mouth even wider in a long drawn out hiss. The foulness of its breath made me gag. I believe I even tried to pray.

And it was then I heard, against all hope, my bedroom door slam back and Father shouting, 'Do you see it, Tadgh?' There was a metallic gleam in the moonlight as his unsheathed sabre whistled through the air and took off its head.

Its twitching body collapsed, a thick black ichor oozing from the neck. Father stamped on its head half a dozen times or more shattering it into viscous fragments. He turned to the still twitching body (which even though headless was trying to rise) and hacked it into flinders with his sabre. He re-lit the lamp and I now saw that what I'd taken for rags were strips of dry leathery skin hanging off fragments of bone.

Father placed a hand on my shoulder which I angrily shrugged off. 'I knew the only way to destroy it was to lure it here. I had no choice,' he said quietly.

'But I thought we'd…'

He cut across me, 'Destroyed it already? No we only drove it out of its nest. It conjured up the storm and escaped to another bolt hole under the cover of darkness. I knew it might lie low for weeks, months even; perhaps move to another district and start all over again. It was gaining in strength. The blood of animals would soon not be enough. Its next victims would have been human.'

Tadgh had so far remained silent but now he stepped forward and said, 'Your father's right. We had no choice but to let it track you back here.'

I was puzzled. 'How did it manage to do that? Did it follow us?'

'Do you remember the second stone you dropped down the well? The one that didn't splash,' Father asked quietly.

'Yes,' I replied warmly, 'Of course I do. What of it?'

'You'd held it before you dropped it and the reason it didn't splash was because it never reached bottom. It was caught by that thing and it had your scent on it. When I saw the finger-marks on your windowpane and you told me of your sudden compulsion to lean over and look down the well, about the moth and the shape by the hedgerow that night, I knew it had tracked you here.'

'But then why didn't it attack that night? Why wait?'

'It couldn't get in. Your window was firmly shut and the sound of breaking glass would have awoken you and roused the house.'

I looked across at my open window and then at him. 'You left it open. It was a clear invitation.' And here I paused before going on angrily, 'And unless I'm very much mistaken you drugged my brandy.' I was numb with shock and looked angrily at both father and Tadgh. 'You used me like a tethered goat in a tiger trap!'

'Just a drop or two of laudanum; I needed you...' Here he paused. 'Docile. If you'd awoken too soon the trap would have been prematurely sprung and our quarry may very well have fled and not returned. It was a calculated risk.'

I could feel my anger receding. What he said made sense but I was still smarting with resentment at being used. 'Why was I unable to move and yet both of you were?'

Tadgh and Father both opened their jackets to reveal crosses hanging around their necks. 'A cross will not destroy one of these creatures but it will nullify some of its power.'

Once I'd finally calmed down, we gathered up the remains in an old pillowcase, took them out into the farmyard and burned them; and then never spoke of it again.

As Holmes finished his story our clock chimed the half-hour and he cut off my, 'Do you really expect me to believe...' with, 'It's late and I've kept you up long enough. Goodnight, Watson and a Merry Christmas to you. Sleep well."

I bid him goodnight and returned his Merry Christmas before retiring. As I lay down I could hear a faint tapping of rain on my bedroom window. Despite the fact that Holmes had begun by assuring me that everything I was about to hear was the truth, I could not shake off the feeling that I was the butt of a joke and as a result did not sleep well that night.

Watson was right; Holmes was making a joke on him.

He tells Watson at 11:45 p.m. that everything he says for the next quarter of an hour will be the absolute truth. He engages Watson in a brief argument about Science and the Paranormal, refills his pipe (and takes his time about it) and then describes his train journey home and meeting with his father. Watson tells us that Holmes' voice had a hypnotic quality: *'Once caught in his spell, the world faded and time passed elsewhere.'*

Just as he reaches the point where the story becomes a fantasy, the clock strikes twelve and *Watson was anxious to hear the rest of Holmes' narrative and only vaguely aware of the clock chiming the hour as he continued.*

End Note

I had no idea when I started to write down my first dream how this project would develop, gather pace and eventually conclude. Contributions from Eire, The Netherlands, India, Kyrgyzstan, America, Siberia, Germany, France, Australia, Romania, Russia and from the UK arrived and whether a poem, a surreal moment, a truth or a comment, all had to be marshalled into a book and you, the reader, have reached the end, but not quite.

This is not the work of a pavement street artist. (He declares his work is all his own.) None of my contributors sought financial recompense. And all royalties from the sale of the book will go to The Alzheimer's Society (United against Dementia).

I now leave you with a short poem to reflect on our human ability to read, write and dream.

A heron in the river Nith
Was lonely in November
His mate was nowhere to be found
Because he couldn't remember.
It's not just folk who have bad days
When everything's forgotten
All creatures are the same as us
And think it's really rotten.
Now I've provoked a truth not known
Well, hardly ever said
Because us folks unlike the fauna
Are just more widely read.
And as our dreams are often dreamt
Does the heron not dream too?
I suspect the fauna dream as well
Like cats and dogs, don't you?

The end.

Sleep tight and enjoy your dreams. Or as I recall telling our young daughters: Sound sleep and sweet repose, sleep on your back, so you don't squash your nose!

Lightning Source UK Ltd.
Milton Keynes UK
UKHW020329221022
410892UK00011B/152